Woman to Woman

Woman to Woman

EQUIPPING YOU TO EMPOWER OTHERS

CWR

Copyright © CWR 2012

Published 2012 by CWR, Waverley Abbey House, Waverley Lane, Farnham, Surrey GU9 8EP, UK. Registered Charity No. 294387. Registered Limited Company No. 1990308.

The rights of Jeannette Barwick, Rosalyn Derges, Gail Dixon, Jane Follett, Lynn Penson and Elaine Storkey to be identified as the authors of their named parts of this work have been asserted by them in accordance with the Copyright, Designs and Patents Act 1988, sections 77 and 78.

For the list of our National Distributors visit www.cwr.org.uk/distributors

Unless otherwise indicated, all Scripture references are from the Holy Bible: New International Version (NIV), copyright © 1973, 1978, 1984 by the International Bible Society. Other versions used: NIV 2011: copyright 1979, 1984, 2011 by Biblica, formerly International Bible Society. All rights reserved. Anglicised edition first published in Great Britain 1979, by Hodder & Stoughton, an Hachette UK company. This revised and updated edition published 2011.
NKJV: *New King James Version*, © 1982, Thomas Nelson Inc.
NLT: Holy Bible New Living Translation, © 1996. Used by permission of Tyndale House Publishers Inc.
TLB: *The Living Bible*, © 1971, 1994, Tyndale House Publishers
The Message: Scripture taken from *The Message*. Copyright © 1993, 1994, 1995, 1996, 2000, 2001, 2002. Used by permission of NavPress Publishing Group.

Concept development, editing, design and production by CWR

Cover image: getty/John Cumming

Printed in Finland by Bookwell

ISBN: 978-1-85345-742-5

CONTENTS

BIOGRAPHIES

Lynn Penson

Lynn has brought her background in theology, education, counselling and Myers-Briggs® personality type training to her role as a tutor for CWR, along with her experience of RE teaching, lecturing at Bible college and various roles within her local church. She leads CWR's Ministry to Women, Myers-Briggs®-related courses and (alongside her husband Andrew) marriage enrichment courses, and she is also involved in CWR's pastoral care courses.

* * * * * * * * * * * *

Jeannette Barwick

Jeannette, founder of CWR's Ministry to Women, has long been committed to helping women around the world apply biblical truths to their lives and relationships, through seminars, books and mentoring. Involved in the life of her local Methodist Church, she is on the Leadership Team and particularly enjoys participating in Fresh Expressions of worship with young families in the community. Jeannette has two married daughters and treasures time with them and her five grandchildren.

* * * * * * * * * * * *

Elaine Storkey

Dr Elaine Storkey, President of Tearfund and member of the Church of England's General Synod, is a well-known Christian academic and broadcaster. A respected theologian and sociologist, she is often to be heard at conferences and on national radio, relating a Christian perspective to twenty-first-century living. She is Director of Education for Church of England Evangelists (Church Army) Chair of the Church and Media Network, and ambassador for Restored - a global Christian initiative against violence to women. A prolific author, Elaine has written six books and hundreds of articles for newspapers and journals. She lectures to postgraduates on the Christian Mind Course at Oxford University.

Rosalyn Derges

Rosalyn trained as a primary school teacher and later as a counsellor with CWR which opened up the potential of teaching on the Introduction to Biblical Counselling as well as the Woman to Woman courses. She works with her husband in a local church in Bridgnorth and has a passion to see women understand who they are in God and to take hold of their position in Him.

* * * * * * * * * * * *

Gail Dixon

Gail is the director of Nations, a mission-planting work, helping to establish and nurture indigenous mission movements in Asia and Africa. She met the Lord as a student, and has been involved in mission work for more than thirty years. Based at the Nations HQ in South Wales, she also leads Celebration for the Nations, a worship movement. She believes that the first command, to love God, and the second, to love our neighbour, can be summed up in worship and mission.

* * * * * * * * * * * *

Jane Follett

Jane and her family have been part of the large, lively Anglican church of Christ the King in Kettering for the last twenty years. Following many years of teaching, bringing up her four children and leading or helping with youth work, she responded to her vicar's invitation to develop Women's Ministry in the church seven years ago. Building on previous good foundations, she now has teams that lead Manna – a Bible study group serving 60-plus women aged from 20-80 years, Weft – a community and church evening group, an annual day conference for the wider church, retreats and other events. The rest of the time she makes pots!

INTRODUCTION

Lynn Penson

We live in a world where friendship, good role models and authentic leadership are highly valued, and it is exciting to see groups for Christian women springing up with the desire to nurture these values. Many women want to grow in their own relationship with God, but also wish to encourage others in their personal and spiritual growth.

There are a number of women in our churches who are working with other women. They may be leading a women's Bible study, coming alongside young mums, organising social occasions, running prayer breakfasts, or women's conferences or forming friendships with women who are just starting a journey of faith. Most of this is done on a voluntary basis. It was the vision of Jeannette Barwick, the founder of CWR's women's ministry at Waverley Abbey House, to provide a course which would equip such women for service. Jeannette's vision was brought to fruition when the first Women Ministering to Women course was run over eight Mondays in 2005. In 2010 this changed to a one-week Woman to Woman training course to enable people from further afield to attend, and it has brought women from many continents as well as from all corners of the UK to study together. The aims are to help them find their personal vision, explore their gifts, develop their skills, increase their confidence, and give tools to help them develop their ministry.

Though many women have been able to benefit from the training, it is still not possible for all who would enjoy the teaching to attend a course at Waverley. This book has been written with those women in mind. We have taken many of the topics covered and invited women to contribute chapters in areas of their expertise and experience.

As you read, take time to think about the various topics and questions, and come to your own conclusions. In order to help you think through the material for yourself, there are suggestions for reflection along the way; use them to get the most out of the material.

A personal world-view

Before embarking on such a study, it is a good exercise to consider what preconceptions we bring. As women sharing an evangelical position and wanting to be faithful to Scripture, we may believe that we will all have the same view about God, the world, the Bible and other topics. However, that is not the case. We all come with our own world-view which has been formed by what we have seen, experienced and thought. Our world-view may be described as our basic philosophy of life – the fundamental beliefs that shape the way we think, live, choose and act; this will shape the way we understand God, the universe and people.

If we understand what we believe and why we believe it, we will understand more fully why and how our beliefs are different from those of other people, and why we react in certain ways. This is a good starting point for working with people of any age and gender. Recognising that we will have different fundamental beliefs and ideas will give us the opportunity to relate to others in a way that is appropriate for them, not expecting them always to be in agreement with us. It also encourages us to consider what we believe and why we believe it, so that we do not fall into the trap of simply accepting what other people say with the inherent dangers accompanying that, but we come to a clear position about our own beliefs and values. This helps us to respect and value both ourselves and others. And that provides a good foundation for working with both women and men.

I am indebted to the people who have taught on the course over the years, and to those who have now contributed to this book. It is always such a privilege and joy to work alongside women who want to serve God, and these women have done this by giving their talents and gifts to invest in others by sharing their knowledge and experience in what they have written.

Our prayer is that you will be encouraged, inspired, equipped and empowered as you serve God and the women in your churches and communities.

Lynn Penson
January 2012

PART 1:

Foundations —
The Big Picture

A BIBLICAL MODEL FOR MINISTRY

Jeannette Barwick

In secular education great use is made of the word 'model' when teaching certain disciplines. But how do we relate that concept to Christian ministry?

Some focus on some of the great personalities of the Old Testament, such as Moses, Ruth and Esther, or prophets like Elijah, and Jeremiah, who was the very picture of faithfulness and fidelity. The Old Testament has many reports of people who stand out as great men and women of God, who served the Lord in their day.

Yet others look at the New Testament apostles. There was Peter, and of course Paul; extraordinary men, their lives filled with characteristics from which we can draw great inspiration. Ultimately, though, our greatest 'model' is Christ Himself. Our Saviour came not to be ministered to, but to minister to others. In Luke 22: 27 He said, 'I am among you as one who serves.'

However, here I want to focus on what I have found to be the most exciting model for ministry to be found anywhere in Scripture – the Trinity.

The Trinity

The truth of the Holy Trinity, whilst accepted by most Bible-believing Christians, is not always clearly understood, so here is a definition given by Selwyn Hughes, the founder of CWR: 'There is more than one divine person in the courts of heaven. God is His own community, made up of three persons, Father, Son and Holy Spirit. Each member of the Trinity has the same status and are co-equal and co-eternal.' The term 'Trinity' does not appear in the Bible; nonetheless, its roots are firmly embedded in Scripture. The Bible begins, 'In the beginning *God*' (Gen. 1:1, my italics). The Hebrew word used is 'Elohim'. It is plural, suggesting there is more than one divine Person in the Godhead. Then in verse 26 we read, 'Let us make man in our image'. Further into the Old Testament there are hints at the plurality in the Godhead. For instance, Isaiah, in his vision in chapter 6 hears the voice of God saying, 'who will go for us?' (v.8) and then there is the triple invocation, 'Holy, holy, holy' (v.3).

In Old Testament times the Trinity was veiled, and it is not until the New Testament that it becomes clear. When Jesus came, His disciples noticed He accepted worship as His right and He forgave sins, something God alone could do. But it was after He rose from the dead that the reality of it hit them. Thomas was the first to express it when he said, 'My Lord and my God!' (John 20:28).

In John 15:26, Jesus talked to His disciples about another Person who would come as comforter and counsellor, and from the earliest days of the Christian Church the three-fold blessing was used: 'the grace of our Lord Jesus Christ, and the love of God and the fellowship of the Holy Spirit' (see 2 Cor. 13:14).

Some years ago, Selwyn Hughes came across this powerful statement by the Australian theologian D. Broughton Knox. Its impact on him was so significant that it had a transforming effect on his whole ministry and is now fundamental to CWR's core teaching. It is taken from the book *The Everlasting God*[1] and expresses the great truth of the Trinity.

> The Father loves the Son and gives Him everything. The Son always does that which pleases the Father. The Spirit takes the things of the Son and shows them to us. We learn from the Trinity that relationship is the essence of reality and therefore the essence of our existence. We also learn that the way this relationship

should be expressed is by concern for others. Within the Trinity itself there is a concern by each person in the Trinity for one another.

The truth is that the Trinity is a community of three Persons *who live in a relationship of pure and endless joy,* where there is no tension, no competitiveness, no arguments, and where each can be themselves without fear of promoting rivalry.

Whoever said 'Two's company; three's a crowd' never did understand the Trinity.

The mind-blowing sentence in that Broughton Knox quotation is the statement, *'relationship* is the essence of reality'.

It is important that several convictions which have developed from the truth of the Trinity are understood by those who long to be used by God in ministering to others.

Pause to reflect

How might you share your belief that the Father, Son and the Holy Spirit are one God to someone who does not believe it? Do you know relevant scriptures, such as Colossian 2:9, Hebrews 1:3? Can you show that the doctrine of the Trinity is clearly portrayed in the Bible, even if the word 'Trinity' is not there?

Truths of the Trinity

The FIRST truth is this – *life is all about relationships.* Someone has said that relationship is the thread out of which God built the universe. Ultimate reality is personal, not propositional. In fact the whole story of the Bible can be spelt out in terms of relationships:

- Perfect relationships in the Trinity
- Broken relationships in Eden
- Restored relationships in Christ.

How many times have you heard someone say, 'I can't live with him/her, or live without him/her'? There's a reason for that.

Encoded in our inner beings is a design feature that marks us out as being made for three kinds of relationships – with others, with ourselves and with God; and these three are inter-related. If one relationship is out of balance, the others will be affected also. Life is all about relationships, and most of the problems you encounter in your own life or in others (if not physical) will have their roots in relationship.

We have all been created by an eternal community of three fully connected Persons, and we bear their image. In connecting with God we gain spiritual life, and in connecting with others we nourish and experience that life. Rugged individualism and independence violate the nature of our existence. The capacities that were given to us that distinguish us as human beings were given so that we could connect – to think, aspire, choose, feel and so on. Connecting with others is as vital to our souls as blood is to our bodies. When it is missing, we are ruled by the need to get it.

We are wired to relate. There are no exceptions.

The SECOND truth we can draw from the Trinity is this: *a good relationship is when we use our resources for the well-being of another.* Remember what Broughton Knox said: 'We also learn that the way this relationship should be expressed is by concern for others. Within the Trinity itself there is a concern by each person in the Trinity for one another.' Clearly, the energy that pulses in the heart of the Trinity is *other-centred.* It is the way it has been from all eternity. Fourth-century theologians painted a picture of God they hoped would give people a vision of what it would mean to fellowship and be in communion with Him. They came up with an interesting Greek word, '*perichoresis*' which literally means to dance around. '*Peri*' means around (from which we get the word 'perimeter') and '*choresis*' (from which we get the word 'choreography') means dance. The Trinity, they suggested, could be properly envisioned as dancing together in the perfect rhythm of love at a wildly exuberant party. The Father dotes on the Son, the Son on the Father, the Spirit also, each pouring into the others their joy and delight at being in this eternal fellowship. Other-centredness is one of the chief characteristics of the Trinity.

To see the importance of this it is helpful to consider for a moment the opposite of other-centredness – self-centredness. Self-centredness is a violation of everything that God has designed. Made in the image of the Trinity, we are built to give ourselves to others in the way the Trinity give themselves to each other. Adam and Eve's sin has damaged our God-made personalities so much, however, that instead of being *Christo*-centric (the way we were designed to be) we have become *ego*-centric. We are at the centre of our lives, rather than Christ. If you could extract self-centredness out of the human soul, humanity would have few personal problems.

The Gospel story can be presented in this way: all three members of the Trinity long to draw others into their joyous and endless dance of other-centredness – their *perichoresis*. The Trinity became engaged in creating a universe in which beings such as you and I could be drawn into a relationship with them and join in the eternal dance. But sin intruded into the picture, and in order to overcome that, the second Person of the Trinity, Jesus Christ, the Son, had to temporarily leave His home in heaven, come to this earth, die on a cross, be raised from the dead, return to heaven, take up His place there once again, and open up the way whereby redeemed sinners can join in the eternal joy that characterises the home of the Father, Son and Spirit. Our Lord Jesus Christ has modelled for us what other-centredness – the hallmark of the Trinity – looks like when demonstrated through a human form. He put the concerns of others ahead of His own. It is only when self-centredness dies in us that Christ can live in us and our relationships become other-centred.

The THIRD truth that the Trinity teaches us is that this *heavenly relationship is one of great passion.* We get a fascinating glimpse in the Gospels of the Father's passion for the Son as He lived out His life on earth. The Gospels record three occasions during Christ's earthly life when the Father spoke directly to the world concerning His Son.

The first is in Matthew 3:13–17 – the absorbing moment when Christ was baptised in the Jordan by John the Baptist. For the first thirty years of Christ's life, the Father had not spoken from heaven. Now here is Jesus rising up out of the waters of baptism, a man who had never sinned. At this moment the Spirit of God came down in the form of a dove, and so our Triune God was revealed to those who were present as they heard the Father overcome with emotion shout out with delight: 'This is my Son, whom I love.' What passion and pride swept through the Father's heart as He saw the life He wanted men and women to live being demonstrated by His beloved Son.

We can put a great deal of emphasis on obedience in the evangelical world (and, of course, that is right), but too little emphasis on the fact of spiritual passion. Our obedience must become an expression of our deepest passions. We need to understand our spiritual journey as a journey of passion, not just one of rule-keeping and obedience which may appear so joyless.

The second time God's voice came from heaven was when Christ was on the Mount of Transfiguration in Matthew 17:5. Again God says 'This is my Son, whom I love', then He adds, 'Listen to him!' Hear the Father's heartbeat.

The third occasion when God spoke is recorded in John 12:20–36, when some Greeks sought out Jesus. Jesus prayed to His Father, 'Father, glorify your name!' and God says, 'I have glorified it, and will glorify it again.' The passion that the Father had for the Son must rule our lives also, if we are to be effective ministers to others.

The FOURTH truth to come to us out of the Trinity is that *only as we engage with the members of this eternal community can we truly and effectively minister to others.* Little can be achieved in the lives of those we attempt to minister to unless what pours out of us into them comes not from us but from the Father, Son and Holy Spirit.

The apostle Paul in Colossians 1:28–29 uses a rather striking phrase when he talks about his ministry to others. He says, 'We proclaim him, admonishing and teaching everyone with all wisdom, so that we may present everyone perfect in Christ. To this end I labour, struggling with all his energy, which so powerfully works in me.'

Clearly, when Paul ministered to others, he experienced an energy flowing out of him that was not his own but was in fact *the energy of Christ.*

In his letter to the Galatians, Paul says, 'My dear children, for whom I am again in the pains of childbirth until Christ is formed in you' (Gal. 4:19). It is clear that Paul had two things – one, a clear vision for the spiritual formation of the people to whom he ministered, and two, a sense that Christ was being poured out of him as he engaged with the men and women he came across in the course of his ministry. Something supernatural was at work. It would be true to say that some help can be given to people when we relate to them on a natural level with earthly wisdom and so on, but what brings about real change (in terms of spiritual growth and development) is *supernatural power*. No one can speak with authority into a person's soul without supernatural power.

This means that there has to be recognition of our inadequacy, and a willingness to draw close to Jesus in deeper communion and fellowship. One thing is sure – we will never be able to stir up the passion in others for Jesus Christ unless it is flowing in us first.

Pause to reflect

Do you have a real passion for Christ in your heart? Are you engaged with the eternal community of the Trinity so that you overflow with love, passion and power to minister to others?

Dance steps of the Trinity

A popular TV programme in the UK is *Strictly Come Dancing*, where celebrities are paired with professional dancers and learn various dance steps. Many of the celebrities who have taken part say they will carry on dancing now they have discovered it's such an enjoyable and engaging experience. The rhythm for ministry which flows out of a passion for Jesus Christ is already in you. You need to learn the steps. It will flow only out of a humble and willing heart. No one dances the waltz right away. They learn a few steps, one movement at a time, and then keep at it until it becomes a graceful rhythm. Ministering to others in a spiritual way is an encounter with a supernatural purpose. To keep in step with other people we need to learn the dance steps of the Trinity, or else we will dance into other people's lives and teach them steps that do not harmonise with the dance of the Father, Son and Holy Spirit.

If you are a follower of Jesus and you have committed your life to

Him, then your soul is alive with God. The actual life of the Trinity is flowing through you at this moment. That life can come out of your words, your tone of voice. There is a passion and energy within you waiting to be released. The rhythm of the Spirit is there in you now – the Spirit who took up residence in your soul when you were born into God's family.

There is a river of life pressing through us. It is a language with a supernatural passion and wisdom in the service of a supernatural purpose. We can spend time focusing on the words, but we must see there is a language of the Spirit that took up residence in our souls when we were born again. Every time you minister to another soul, it's as though you are walking on to the dance floor with a rhythm that is already inside you. You just need to have the humility to learn a few important dance steps.

What are you seeking to do when you engage with another person? What is your vision? Surely it is to know God better. The passion in our hearts for others is that, like Paul, we see people become mature in Christ. We dialogue when the words we utter are formed by the passion to see another person want God more than anything else, and by the wisdom of the Spirit, with only the prayer that God will use our words. There ought to be no power struggle in the ministry of helping others.

If the Holy Spirit is not at work, then not much will be accomplished.

If you are willing to live with an honest awareness of inadequacy, and are willing to struggle with a whole host of strange feelings, then you are ready for the task. There is a wonderful verse in the Living Bible: '[God's] power shows up best in weak people' (2 Cor. 12:9) – or as the NIV has it, 'my power is made perfect in weakness'.

The truth of the Trinity suggests to us that God wants us to learn the steps of the eternal dance in which the Father, Son and Spirit engage us, and teach those steps to others. And what are those steps? *Relationships matter.* Unless we relate well to God, ourselves and others, then life will be fraught with problems.

Other-centredess is another step. Our lives must be lived in such a way that our concerns for others exceed our concerns for ourselves.

Another of the steps is a *focus on Jesus*. The biggest issue in the heart of the Trinity is to make us more and more like Jesus Christ. The Living Bible says: 'For from the very beginning God decided that [we] ... should become like His Son' (Rom. 8:29). God is so excited about Jesus that He wants to make everyone else like Him. The Spirit's work is to make us more like Christ, never forget that. When the life of God in me touches the life of God in another, it is wonderful. We are called to pour something of Christ into others, to touch something deep in them and to teach them the first steps that can help them engage in the dance with the Trinity.

When you are involved in ministry to others, the main thing that should be on your mind is, 'How can I engage with the Trinity in such a way that I can learn the dance steps that I can teach to others? How can I talk with someone in ways that arouse their passion for God and His Son, Jesus Christ? How can I help them discover what they really want – an intimate passionate relationship with Christ? How can I speak a language that helps to pull back the curtains of their souls and show them how to enter into that eternal dance?'

Pause to reflect

Think about that last paragraph. You may wish to make it a prayer.

I love Graham Kendrick's song, *Teach me to dance to the beat of Your heart, teach me to move in the power of Your Spirit* ...[2] Whenever I sing it, I think of this Trinitarian approach to ministry. The words beautifully express the desire to learn the rhythm of life as God intended. I encourage you to open your heart to connect with Jesus. Allow yourself to fall more deeply in love with Him than ever before. The love relationship in the Trinity is the model for the universe, and it is our model for love, our model for life and for ministry.

NOTES
1. David Broughton Knox, *The Everlasting God* (Darlington: Evangelical Press, 1982).
2. Graham Kendrick and Steve Thompson (c) 1993. Make Way Music.
    www.grahamkendrick.co.uk Used by permission.

THE BIBLICAL PLACE OF WOMEN

Elaine Storkey

Introduction

Over the years much has been written about the Bible and women, often with different messages. This should not surprise us. When we explore the teaching of the Bible in any area of our lives, we do not come to the biblical text neutrally. Because we are relational beings and have to make sense of life in our own era and context, inevitably we bring to the text a multitude of traditions, attitudes, church policies and social habits. However, this does not mean that the Bible is unreliable in any way. It simply means that, as humans, we have limitations and do not always get things right.

In the case of slavery, for example, history demonstrates that more than a century of debate over law and biblical interpretation took place before its subsequent abolition. Why? Because Christian people in North America and elsewhere accepted slavery as a 'normal' part of society. After all, didn't St Paul instruct slaves to obey their masters (Eph. 6:5–8)? It was not until people recognised the depths of biblical teaching that attitudes changed; Paul gave this advice to slaves for the wellbeing and unity of the Church in a *specific* context and against the background of the practices of those times. But his deeper vision was expressed in Galatians 3:28 where he affirmed that the old barriers between people – old ways of endorsing privileges and denying freedom to others – must be abolished:

'There is neither Jew nor Greek, slave nor free, male nor female, for you are all one in Christ Jesus.' By it, he expressed that, ultimately, there can be no slavery – it is wrong to uphold the dominance of the powerful and exploit the vulnerability of the weak.

Equally susceptible to debate is the biblical teaching on gender and women. Throughout history, there has repeatedly been great controversy over what roles women should occupy – in the family, the Church, at work – and whether they should be in leadership.

Bringing assumptions with us

I have already stated that we need to be aware of the assumptions which we bring with us when we read the Bible. It is so easy to read our own attitudes back into the text, or interpret it through our own experience alone. This can distort what any passage is saying and even lead the Church into practices which do not reflect the biblical message.

I can illustrate the importance of this most effectively by taking an example from an early theologian. St Jerome, who translated the Bible into the Latin 'Vulgate' (the key biblical translation used for centuries by the Catholic Church) also greatly influenced the Church's ideas of women and sexuality. St Jerome spent much of his life in disciplined contemplation and scholarship, but also, I suspect, in fear of women's sexuality. This is evidenced by letters which he wrote to young women who sought his pastoral advice. In them, he advised against accepting offers of betrothal because he felt that a life without sex was far better than marriage. So strong was this belief that he finds it justified even, at the very beginning of the Bible. In his commentary on the first book of Genesis, he argued that:

> There is something not good in the number two ... This
> we must observe, at least if we would faithfully follow the
> Hebrew that while Scripture on the first, third, fourth
> and sixth days relates that, having finished the works
> of each, God saw that it was good, on the second day
> He omitted this altogether, leaving us to understand

that two is not a good number because it prefigures the marriage contract.[1]

At best, such exegesis is strange; at worst, it is distorted and biased. Jerome leaps from an observation about God's pleasure with creation to the absurd suggestion that God is not in favour of marriage! And he concludes this from the fact that, because God does not repeat how good everything is on the second day, there must be something wrong with the implications of 'two' – which must be its implicit allusion to sexual intercourse! It is extraordinary – all the more so because it suggests that sex is so uppermost in his mind that he even reads it into the days of creation! And sadly, his opinions left their mark on attitudes in the Church towards women and sexuality for generations.

Sexuality and biology

Behind this strange way of reading Genesis is a view that sexuality and biology are central to understanding the nature of women. Unfortunately, it was not exclusive to St Jerome. Today, people still argue that the biological and sexual differences between women and men produce 'hard-wiring' in us which affects us in every area of life. Differences in the chromosomal structure of male and female are echoed by differences in anatomy, physiology, hormones, reproductive organs, weight, disposition and brain use. These are all played out in the way we exhibit different kinds of physical strength ('horsepower' against stamina and endurance) or life expectancy (women have greater longevity).

Biological differences are also tied to the process of procreation, where men produce the sperm, and women the egg, but women give birth and feed their young. It is easy to understand people then, when they state that these differences in biology fit the sexes for different roles in society. Men are hard-wired for jobs where independence and risk are necessary. Women are designed for roles of nurturing. Biology has been offered as an explanation for even emotional and intellectual differences between the sexes.

Yet that conclusion is questionable. No one doubts that there are biological differences between women and men, but it is less easy to say with certainty what these differences mean in social relations. Unfortunately, this does not stop writers of popular books on the male and female from staking strong claims. In *Why Men don't Iron* for example, the authors see biology as an explanation for everything.[2] Consider, for example, their claims about competitiveness:

> A man enjoys a neurological high when he is faced by competition ... a woman is not equipped by biology to receive this neurological reward. Indeed, if anything, her reaction to competition will be anxiety.[3]

These words seem to intimate the view that men can tolerate competition, women cannot; women should remain at home whilst men go out as the bread-winners engaging in competitive activity. Such a view is echoed by the authors' references to housework, likewise seen as 'women's work' because:

> Man has a lower sensitivity to detail, which means he simply does not notice the dust as she does ... the stale socks and sweaty shirt don't bother him because they are among the pheromone-related smells that women are acutely aware of, but men do not detect.[4]

Even more alarming, this same appeal to biological difference is offered as a justification of infidelity:

> Some high testosterone-level males do marry, but they are 43 per cent more likely to be divorced and 38 per cent more likely to engage in extramarital sex ... The conclusion seems obvious. You can have a man, but you cannot have a man who feels, touches, cares and empathises like a woman, not if you want him to stay a man.[5]

Not only is this particular statement dangerous and amoral, it is also unscientific, despite the authors' claim that their book is a scientific account of gender. In fact, few scientific studies test the testosterone levels of men engaged in extra-marital sex to draw such a specific conclusion.

Ultimately, the problems with the claims in this book are almost too obvious to state. The authors make many assumptions and the scientific nature of the explanation is overstated but little evidence is given. More importantly, the authors reduce our complex human personhood – with its spiritual, emotional, mental, familiar, historical, linguistic, ethnic and cultural influences – simply to biology which is then offered as an explanation for everything. The weaknesses of this approach are evident. Biology certainly plays a key role in our lives, yet we are much more than our biology.

Biology and theology

Particularly unsettling is when biological reductionism enters Christian discourse about men and women. But it does. Over the years, several theologians have claimed that, since God created men and women biologically different, He did so for a purpose: women should be homemakers, and men should be leaders. This is strongly articulated by Larry Christenson, whose book *The Christian Family* was once regarded as a Christian classic on the subject of the family:

> If a father spends time in traditional, biological female tasks, such as child-care or basic nurture – feeding the children and dressing them – it produces problems for the next generation. Their sons may well grow up not knowing what it means to be a man.[6]

However this is loaded with assumptions, not least about the link between tradition and biology and what it is to be a man. In fact, we could argue that sons whose fathers have cared for them at a young age may well grow up to be very secure men – because they have been brought up by fathers who don't feel afraid about being involved in mundane roles for their children!

Some theologians even put biology and spirituality side by side.

William Oddie, a minister who left the Church of England over the decision to ordain women to the priesthood wrote:

> It is a clear and consistent assumption that biological differences correspond to differences of spiritual identity.[7]

This may be a 'consistent assumption', but that does not mean it is well-founded. It is very difficult to know how we would identify 'biologically based spiritual identity'. In fact, it is little but a very sweeping generalisation. Yet the theme is taken up elsewhere. A former bishop of London, Graham Leonard, pointed to 'spiritual' differences when he insisted in an unpublished lecture that:

> The whole world knows that men are associated with giving and women with receiving.

This might sound like upside-down thinking; the whole world knows that women are very much the givers. Throughout history, they have given to men, to other women, to families and to children, often generously and without counting the cost. So why does the Bishop get it so wrong? The answer is that he cannot get beyond biology and sex, where the man is indeed the giver and the woman is the receiver for, biologically, the man 'gives' the sperm to the woman. Yet we cannot make that into the universal defining point about the fundamental roles of men and women without denying history!

The difference between sex and gender

The problem with all these claims is that, ultimately, biology is being offered as a *universal* explanation and it seeps into the way we understand gender, creation, society, history and spirituality. It also influences how we read the Bible. It fails to distinguish between two key concepts – sex and gender – and therefore confuses what can be explained by biology and what is really related to culture.

When we look at these different concepts more carefully (outlined in the lists opposite) we gain a better understanding of the influences that operate in the lives of women and men.

SEX	GENDER
• Male or female	• Man or woman
• Biological category	• Cultural category
• Identify scientifically	• Identify socially
• Chromosomes, genes, anatomy, physiology, hormones, brain use	• Roles, expectations, work, communication, learning, upbringing, class
• Reproductive, genital	• Not fixed, flexible
• Same in all cultures	• Cultural variations

Sex offers us relatively little choice – we receive our sexuality as a given, we procreate, urinate, give birth and lactate in ways appropriate to our sex organs. And this happens irrespective of culture, language, customs or even the time in which we live. Our bodies behave according to the creation plan which God has built into us, and which exists also in other parts of creation. Where we *do* have a choice is in how we live out our sexuality in a moral and spiritual context: for then it becomes gender.

Gender is related to culture and social practice and offers us much more choice. We *learn* how to behave as men and women, not simply following a *biological* pattern, but in ways which are *socially* acceptable. And when we look at the jobs women and men hold, or the different way they are treated in societies, it is rarely accounted for by differences in sex or biology. It is much more likely to be related to the gender assumptions, power and expectations which have become engrained in public consciousness, including in the Church.

The distinction between sex and gender clearly has many implications. Views about biology are often tied into views about hierarchy. And those Christians who fail to distinguish between sex and gender will also fail to see that we do not in fact 'unsex' women by releasing them into certain roles. People who believe that women and men are strongly determined by their biological make-up are also more likely to believe that the Bible teaches hierarchy rather

than equality in their relationships. It is to this that we now need
to turn.

A question of hierarchy or equality

The debate about hierarchy and equality has overshadowed almost
all others in relation to the Bible and women. Those who hold a
hierarchical view have often claimed that their view alone is the
biblical one, and focus their case on a number of passages or ideas
including:

1. The order of creation – because Adam was formed first, man
   should have authority over women (Gen. 2:21–23)
2. The designation of Eve as *ezer* – 'helpmeet' suggests that women
   are inferior or subordinate to men (Gen. 2:18)
3. Male leadership is found throughout the Old Testament
4. The twelve disciples chosen by Christ were all male (Matt. 10:2–4)
5. Paul's teaching at Corinth – women should be silent in the
   Church and defer to their husbands(1 Cor. 14:34–36)
6. The concept of 'headship' – the husband is described as the
   'head of the wife'(Eph. 5: 22–24)
7. Paul's instructions to Timothy – women should not be permitted
   to exercise authority over men (1 Tim. 2:12)
8. The teachings on 'wifely submission' and obedience
9. The assumption that male leadership is the preference
   throughout the New Testament

It is easy to have sympathy for the claims of those who see hierarchy
here and draw the conclusion that the responsibility of leadership is
given to men, whereas women are to be subordinate. When we put
these passages together, the differences between women and men
in the Bible seem to outweigh the ways in which they are similar.

However, there are also other passages which suggest a much
more egalitarian and mutual view of the sexes and many biblical
scholars would argue that this is certainly the position which is
taken in the New Testament. They would point to the following:

1. The fact that many Old Testament women were prophets
2. Deborah was a woman with recognised leadership qualities – both a prophet and a judge in Israel (Judg. 4–5)
3. Christ repeatedly included women in His teaching and examples (Matt. 9:18–25; 12:46–49; 15:21–28 etc)
4. Jesus specifically affirmed Mary Magdalene, a well-known prostitute who did not fit the stereotypical female role (Matt. 26:6–13)
5. The resurrection appearances to women (Matt. 28:1–10; Mark 16:1–10; Luke 24:1–10; John 20:10–18)
6. The four daughters of the evangelist Philip were prophets (Acts 21:9)
7. Paul advocates mutuality rather than hierarchy in marriage (1 Cor. 7)
8. Priscilla was a woman who openly taught and evangelised men (Acts 18:26; Rom. 16:3)
9. Women like Junias were leaders in the Early Church (Rom. 16)

With such a range of passages available we would do well to note an observation from Clare Powell: 'The curious thing is that the source for these widely differing views is precisely the same text. The text itself faces us with choices more complex than merely to take or leave it.' This certainly challenges the view that either you hold a hierarchical position or you ignore Scripture.

So what do we do with this debate? Certainly we won't get far if we merely swap texts. I have already commented on how important it is to recognise that we bring cultural assumptions to our reading of the biblical text. If we are to be faithful to the biblical witness, it is crucial therefore that we continue to seek discernment on what is timeless and what is cultural.

We have to recognise, for example, that within the biblical text there are statements which are universally true and those which are time-bound and relevant for a particular culture. Teachings which are universally relevant are truths which make up the bedrock of what Christians believe. They are statements like: God is love; God is the Maker of heaven and earth; God was in Christ, reconciling the world to Himself; those who believe in Christ shall not perish but have eternal life. Hundreds of such statements shape the doctrines of the Church and have defined its beliefs throughout history.

We hold on to these truths in a way that doesn't apply to that host of statements which are time-bound – there for specific periods. Many of those are in the Old Testament – like the laws on hygiene, fasting, clothing, lending or gleaning. The deeper principles behind them may be significant, and appropriate today, but the actual instructions are tailored for particular cultures long past. Even in the New Testament there are passages which we now regard as not relevant for us – like prohibitions about eating strangled meat, wearing veils or banning the circumcision of Gentile believers. We take note, and look for what these passages might be saying to us today, but we do not transpose them into our own culture and they do not define what we believe.

It is also important to set the debate within a bigger framework; to see the difficult passages we encounter within the context of the unfolding story of God's relationship with us, His creation and the world in which we live. To do this, it is helpful to consider the four main themes commonly used by biblical scholars: Creation, Sin, Redemption and Pentecost.

Creation: women and men as created beings

We start with the first great theme of the Bible – creation, and the book of Genesis where God issues big commands 'Let there be!' and calls a whole world into being out of nothing. The creation of humans is first mentioned in Genesis 1: 'Let us make man in our image, in our likeness ... So God created man in his own image, in the image of God he created him; male and female he created them' (vv.26–27).

In the second chapter of Genesis this is padded out for us (vv.4–23). The language and scope are different. The chapter is more poetic, gentle and detailed in its descriptions of how God scooped up the dust of the earth and breathed life into someone who became a living human creature. The implication is clear: we are creaturely and share many characteristics with the rest of creation. (Apparently, 95 per cent of our DNA is found in primates and 35 per cent of our

DNA is present in bananas!) However, we are distinct in so far as we are the 'image of God', created in His likeness, and having been given responsibility and stewardship over the rest of creation. So altogether, these verses indicate both the uniqueness of our created humanness and our similarity with the rest of God's creation as well as demonstrating our bi-unity as male and female.

In Genesis 2, we also learn that 'it is not good for the man to be alone' (v.18).

God determines to rectify this situation so He causes Adam to fall into a deep sleep and from the structure of one human being a second, 'woman', is made. Although she is differentiated sexually, the order of creation is not significant here; it is the unity of the sexes that matters. It is significant that God does not go back to the dust of the earth to make a second human creature, but instead, one becomes two. Our sexual difference from each other as male and female is therefore blended with our similarity to each other, and our fundamental unity as fellow human beings. We belong together and need each other. As Adam points out, she is his *isha* ('woman') to his *ish* ('man'). Adam is not naming the woman here, in the way that he previously named the animals – rather, he is giving the generic term for 'woman taken out of man'.

It is here that we note the concept of woman being the 'helpmeet' of man. Contrary to those who read in this idea the notion of woman's subordination, the Hebrew term *ezer* implies something very different. It is used to denote not an inferior, but someone who stands alongside the other. In the twenty-one times in which it is used in the Old Testament, it often carries the sense of power or strength and is generally used of equals.[8] Sometimes it is even used of God, proclaiming Him the strength and power of His people.[9] That is the resonance of the term here. The woman, as *ezer*, is not somebody who has been given to Adam as a subordinate to have authority over but as someone who will walk with Adam in the unity of their humanity. It is reinforced by Adam's cry, 'bone of my bones and flesh of my flesh' (Gen. 2:23) – as if to say: we belong to each other; we are human together!

Understanding gender then through a creation perspective helps us to see more of our humanness. We are created by God, as significant, purposeful, accountable and creaturely. We are dependent on God and transparent before God. We are described as the 'image' of God; and, like God, we are relational; in our humanness we are in union with each other, needing one another. We are also interdependent – made different but similar. We're made for love and compassion, for intimacy and trust. We are unique where we each have individuality, yet we are also communal and need others in our lives. We need people to love us and acknowledge our significance. We are part of creation whilst being the guardians of the rest of creation and charged to seek justice for creation. Ultimately, men and women are loved equally by God; created to be integrated in body, mind, spirit, emotion and made for eternity.

Sin: its impact on women and men

Sadly, the biblical story of our humanness does not end there, and the scene rapidly changes in Genesis 3. The warning given to Adam *not* to eat the forbidden fruit is disregarded and, together, Adam and Eve disobey God. We now see deterioration in their relationship. God calls Adam to account for making this bid for autonomy and going his own way rather than God's. Adam now has a choice how to respond to God. He could admit his sin and show remorse, asking for forgiveness. But a different response is given. In one short reply he effectively shrugs off personal responsibility and blames both the woman and God, claiming 'The woman you put here with me – she gave me some fruit from the tree ...' (v.12).

In Genesis 3 we read too of the consequences of sin: the arduous nature of work, the difficult childbirth, and the male dominance in the relationship between male and female. This is completely absent from the creation story and it is interesting that God states sin will impact the man and the woman in different ways. God says to the woman, 'Your desire will be for your husband and he will rule over you' (v.16). Theologians have argued about what the word 'desire' means, whether it refers to desire for mastery or desire for intimacy. But the consequences are clear enough. Male rule and its effects impact and distort the mutuality and reciprocation of the relationship man and woman were created to have.[10]

Whilst the creation narrative gave us harmony, mutuality, love, openness and transparency, where man, woman and God walked together, the sin narrative brings in subservience, rule and domination. The consequence of our sin is that evil is opened up and begins to affect every part of our human lives, whether in our culture, communities or churches.

Sin has so many negative qualities. It is alienating: cutting us off from God, other people, ourselves, and the rest of creation. Alienation separates us. Sin is also destructive: it tears down and destroys, for it cannot build up. Moreover, sin is distortive. It takes truths, makes them into shady half-truths, quarter-truths, untruths, absolute lies, even complete violations. Sin turns whatever is honest and open into something that's closed and wrong. Worse still, sin is addictive: it controls us and we give ourselves over to it until it takes away our freedom and becomes habitual. Eventually, we can't stop sinning save through the power of the Holy Spirit who breaks that powerlessness in us.

Sin is even structural: it affects societies, and institutions and patterns of governments. It seeps into the way people operate, into the use of money, structures of banking, economics, work and military power. Finally, sin is generational: patterns of stealing, lying, corruption or domestic violence can be transmitted from one generation to another. It is important then to understand the strength and the ubiquity of sin, because it makes us realise how deeply we *need* to be saved from its effects and freed from its relentless grip.

Many of the books of the Hebrew Scriptures deal with stories of sin and disobedience, and serve to emphasise how crucial is God's love and mercy. Sin is shown to be present in gender relations – whether in passages like the cowardice of Abraham (Gen. 21:8–14), the rape of the Levite's concubine (Judg. 19), or the violation of Tamar (2 Sam. 13). Through lies and distortion, manipulation and deceit, lust and sexual violence, we are reminded again and again of the evil men and women are capable of.[11]

Redemption: promised and delivered to all humankind

It is with enormous relief then, that we discover that sin does not have the last word. God's redemption is promised, prophesied in the Old Testament and delivered by Christ in His death for us on the cross. The full weight of the redemptive work of God is enormous and beyond the scope of this chapter. But we need to understand the significance of redemption in relation to women.

Women throughout the biblical narrative demonstrate the power of redemption. For example, the actions of Sarah, Rebekah, Naomi, Ruth, Esther and Rahab all point to the power of God working through women. Likewise, the courage and wisdom of the Hebrew midwives, Shiphrah and Puah, who defied the Pharaoh in not aborting the male children of the women in their care, goes down through history. There were also the amazing women leaders – prophets like Miriam or Hulda, (who interpreted the Book of the Law to the insomniac king and prophesied God's judgement on Israel) or Deborah, the judge described as the 'Mother of all Israel' and whose wisdom and right judgements brought peace to Israel for forty years.

Even though the culture which formed the background of the Hebrew Scriptures was indeed patriarchal, there were numerous moments in its history where we can see the promise of redemption in gender relations. In the Book of Numbers, and later in Chronicles, for example, we read the story of the daughters of Zelophehad who had been excluded from the allocation of land, for their father had no male heirs (Num. 27). They petitioned Moses, Eleazar the priest and the whole Israelite assembly for their right to inherit his property rights instead. Moses took their case to God, and was told that their plea was just. It is an echo of the provisions at the end of the Book of Job, where Job confers the same legacy on his daughters as his sons (Job 42:15). Incidents such as these signify that something visionary was already happening – even before Christ's death on the cross – and it looks towards the redemption of relationships between men and women.

We see this yet more clearly in the prophetic vision of gender inclusion which is given by God to the prophet Joel: 'I will pour out my Spirit on all people. Your sons and your daughters will prophesy, your old men will dream dreams, your young men will see visions. Even on my servants, both men and women, I will pour out my Spirit in those days' (Joel 2:28–29). Through Christ's redemption there will indeed be reconciliation in place of alienation, and the power and love of God will break the chains of addiction, delusion, destruction, distortion and despair. Christ's death for human sin opens the way back to the Father and offers us forgiveness and new life.

It is Christ who brings this redemption into our *human* relationships since He has broken down barriers between people; there is neither Jew nor Greek, slave nor free, male nor female any longer. This redemption of relationships is shown with clarity in the Gospels. There, Jesus frequently cuts across the cultural stereotypes or expectations of women and acts differently. Examples include:

1. He prevents a woman from being stoned to death by the crowd – her partner in adultery is not sharing the punishment with her (John 8:1–11)
2. He uses a generous widow as a role model for His disciples (Luke 21:1–4)
3. He denies men the right to divorce their wives on their own whims (Matt. 19:3–9)
4. He allows the mothers of Salem to bring their children to Him (Mark 10:14–16)
5. He defends Mary who chooses to sit and learn from Him, rather than become obsessed with domestic chores (Luke 10:38–42)
6. He includes women in His parables and makes time for them in His ministry (Luke 15:8–10; 8:1–3)

Whether it is the Samaritan woman at the well, the woman suffering from menstrual abnormalities, or the woman who anoints Him, we see them receive freedom and affirmation in their interaction with Jesus. Not surprisingly, it is women who support His ministry, women who remain at the foot of the cross, women who go to anoint His body and women who are entrusted with the message of resurrection. Jesus shows us both the meaning and outworking of redemption, and honours women in a way that remains a powerful challenge to us in our churches today.

Pentecost: the coming of the Spirit upon women and men

The outpouring of the Spirit seals the redemptive work of the cross. In the Acts of the Apostles, the Early Church experiences the power and release of the Holy Spirit and the ancient prophecies of Joel are realised. Women do indeed receive the Spirit's anointing and move into works of teaching, leading, counselling and prophecy. Philip's four daughters are given a special mention (Acts 21:9) whilst Phoebe takes the letter to the Roman Church and is referred to as a 'deacon' (Rom. 16:1–3) – the same title Paul applies to himself. Junias is named as part of an apostolic couple (Rom. 16:7), Priscilla teaches (Rom. 16:3), Euodia and Syntyche are told not to let their disagreements get in the way of the unity of their leadership (Phil. 4:2), and, altogether, the roll call of women who are active co-workers with Paul occupies a large space in Romans 16.

Difficult passages: applying the interpretative framework

This process of using key biblical themes to develop a hermeneutical framework is very important; through it, I believe we are able to see the issues I raised earlier as part of a bigger picture. We can read Old Testament passages which outline women's subjugation against an interpretive backcloth. For example, take the assumption of male dominance and how it is illustrated in the passage mentioned earlier, Judges 19. Here, the woman has no freedom of choice, even over her sexuality. She has to endure the indifference of the husband as to her safety, and then the horrors of a gang rape and finally murder. We can, with some authority, insist that this is not a 'creation story' which outlines how God intends us to live! Instead, it is a sombre picture of the cycle of sin when people do 'what is right in their own eyes'; the dominance and brutality in it reflect human sin in the depths of our fallen nature, and show the very opposite of how women should be treated. Rather than approval, this behaviour ultimately brings severe judgment from God.

Our principles of interpretation also help us to address the hierarchy and equality debate as it applies to the teachings of St Paul in the New Testament. Paul was living and preaching after the event of Pentecost so his words give us a picture of the kind of redemptive relationships where women and men can be released into the power of the Holy Spirit. However Paul was also very conscious of sin and how that can drag us back into legalism. Galatians 3:28, already quoted twice in this chapter, remains the foundational vision for how he sees those relationships.

It is interesting that Paul chooses three particular divisions in Galatians 3 – slaves, Gentiles and women – for they would be very familiar to a Jewish readership. Some years ago, I was visiting a Jewish synagogue and my host was interpreting the Hebrew readings and prayers for me. I suddenly heard a prayer which I recognised. The man praying was thanking God that he was not a Gentile, slave or a woman! When I remarked upon it to my host he assured me that the prayer carried no disrespect towards Gentiles or women, it was just a great blessing to be born a free, Jewish man, for it carried deep responsibilities. This attitude is exactly what Paul addressed centuries ago in his letter to the Galatians – effectively telling his readers that Jewish free men have no higher status before God than Gentile slave women, because in Christ, barriers are eradicated and we are on level ground. The amazingly radical nature of this has still to penetrate the Church today.

In light of this teaching, we can see that when Paul asks women to 'remain silent in the churches' (1 Cor. 14:34), he is not forbidding women to exercise their gifts, but encouraging orderly worship where women do not break in and disturb the flow of worship. They are asked not to speak (the Greek word *lalein* is usually associated with chatter, or breaking in, inappropriately with 'tongues') and to raise any questions at home with their husbands. To ask women not to distract others by chit-chat or butting in is clearly a very different thing from forbidding them to speak prophetically. The women who were prophets and teachers in the early Church seemed to have received no such rebuke.

Similarly, when Paul asks women to 'submit to their husbands' (Eph. 5:24) we mistakenly think this is the same meaning implied in asking that children obey their parents (Eph. 6:1). However, as with previous cases, the meaning is very different. The word used within marriage does not denote 'obedience', but 'submission' – in other words it is a voluntary requirement. What is more, the submission is mutual; the verb actually comes in Ephesians 5:21 as 'submit to one another out of reverence for Christ. The message is that the whole body of Christ is to be the place where people submit to others – literally, they 'put themselves under', give up their own self-interest for the sake of the other. By this, we can see that Paul is reflecting Jesus' own teaching about not looking out primarily for what *we* want, but being willing to submit to the service of others. In this passage, the husband is described as the head (*kephale*) of the wife, but this word has the connotation of being an enabler, rather than an authority figure (Eph. 5:23). In fact, Paul asks men to 'love [their] wives, just as Christ loved the church' and as they love their own bodies (a tall order!) but he only asks wives to 'respect [their] husband[s]' (Eph. 5:25,33). Yet women of course should also love their husbands, even though Paul does not directly ask them to, just as husbands have sometimes to submit. Love and submission go together, as two halves of the same coin. They are mutual requirements – both for men and women in the outworking of their relationships.

So, where difficult passages ascribed to Paul *seem* contradictory, we need to see them in the light of the deeper underlying principles. We also need to weigh them against Paul's own actions. When women appear to be forbidden to teach in 1 Timothy 2 (*didasko*), we must put this alongside the fact that Priscilla has a teaching ministry in Acts 18 (*didasko*) and it is a ministry clearly endorsed by Paul. Logically, it cannot be a universal prohibition. To use a male example, when Paul circumcises Timothy (whose father was a Gentile) we have to also remember that he insists that Gentiles should not be circumcised. Very often the biblical text demonstrates that Paul goes against his own principles of liberty and freedom in the Church for the greater unity. For not all Christians are mature enough to accept the freedom the Spirit brings and ultimately, his message is that we need to bear with the weaker brothers and sisters.

Conclusion

Any careful and thoughtful attempt at grasping what the Bible says about women and men must recognise that the Bible draws on four concepts which are often polarised. We have seen that it affirms the themes of difference, sameness, complementarity, union. But it holds them together, returning to each of them in different contexts and using them to build up a bigger picture of who we are. And these themes are played out through the great dramas of Creation, Sin, Redemption and Pentecost. Between them, they spell out the meaning of our humanity.

For, we are created *together* as the image of God. *Together,* we have allowed sin to spoil our lives. *Together* we need redemption through the love of Christ and *together* we receive gifts from the Spirit.

There is no gender barrier or hierarchy in the freedom of the Spirit, for it is a freedom to serve and not to dominate. Women and men together are to exhibit the fruit of the Spirit: love, joy, peace, patience, kindness, goodness, faithfulness, gentleness and self-control. They are to exercise gifts of pastoring, teaching, discernment, wisdom, counselling, tongues, prophecy, healing, rebuking, generosity and hospitality. They are to model servant leadership and mutual submission even in cultures which encourages us to put self first. They are to learn to forgive and be forgiven. They are to listen, to reach out with healing and to bring the love of God into broken lives and painful relationships.

The biblical vision for women and men is a radical and demanding confrontation with the structures and attitudes which dominate our world. The real challenge is to live it out.

Pause to reflect

There are examples of women who have had key roles to fulfil throughout both Old and New Testaments. Have you been restrained by perceived cultural limitations as to what you could achieve, rather than following biblical examples? Does this chapter give you a wider vision for your role? Pray through any personal responses.

NOTES

1. St Jerome, *The Tract Against Jovinian* quoted in Jane Barr 'The Influence of St Jerome on Medieval Attitudes to Women' in Janet Martin Soskice, *After Eve* (Collins Marshal Pickering, 1990).
2. Bill and Anne Moir, *Why Men Don't Iron: The Real Science of Gender Studies* (London: HarperCollins, 1998).
3. Ibid p. 255
4. Ibid p. 265
5. Ibid p. 265
6. Larry Christenson, *The Christian Family* (Grand Rapids: Baker Book House, 1970).
7. William Oddie, *What will happen to God* (London: SPCK, 1983).
8. Deut. 33:29
9. See Joseph Coleson Ezer Cenegdo, *A Power like Him: Facing Him as Equal* (Grantham: Philadelphia, Weslyan Holiness, 1996).
10. See the commentary on Genesis 3 in Catherine Clark Kroeger and Mary Evans, *Study Bible for Women* (Oxford: University Press, 2009).
11. For an analysis of some of the passages which describe violence towards women, read Catherine Clark Kroeger and Nancy Nason-Clark, *No Place for Abuse* (Illinois: InterVarsity Press, 2005).

WOMEN AND 21ST-CENTURY CULTURE

Elaine Storkey

Women in our own culture

The past: expectations of women

The movement towards feminism and the societal perceptions of
women we know today did not develop overnight. Just two generations
ago, a woman's place was in the home and most women expected to
marry and have children. In fact, most women did marry and stayed
married to the same person for life. Because the 'public' world (ie the
political and business sphere), was predominantly male and often
hostile towards married women, those who did enter it were either
single or felt they had to choose between motherhood and career.

The division of gender roles also existed within households:
women looked after their husbands and children whilst men
provided the income. Yet this arrangement was not isolating
for women; many people lived within a short distance of their
extended family, and the daily schedule would include visits to
family members. In fact, it was not unusual for families to spend
their entire lives with the same people in the same geographical
context.

When families did move, it was largely for work – that is for the
father's work. For those who moved, the process could be dramatic,
especially for those who faced the adventure of uprooting and
migrating to former colonies like Australia or Canada. After the

First World War, the British Government offered ex-servicemen free passage to one of the dominions or colonies and 17,000 emigrants arrived in Australia between 1919 and 1922. This figure was exceeded more than tenfold in the late 1940s and 1950s when the Assisted Passage Scheme offered cheap passage to Australia at only £10 for an adult and £5 for each teenage child.[1] The tight-knit nature of families meant that whole families often emigrated together, and the wife continued the relationships established in Britain in this new context abroad.

For those who remained in the UK, there were different expectations played out in the distinctions made between educating girls and boys. Gender preference was assumed even in the choice of subject. Advice on science education in the 1950s was particularly patronising towards girls and suggested that science would have to be 'domesticated' before they would show an interest in it. Beyond A-levels, more boys than girls had a university education, especially at Oxford and Cambridge where the ratio of boys to girls was around 10:1. In fact, differences between the sexes were seen as fundamental to education, and they were offered as a justification for social policy. Gender distinctives reinforced the different patterns for work, education and domestic lives.

The earliest feminist groups saw these differences as crippling for women. Their writings and campaigns initially included the slogan 'biology is destiny'. From the 1970s however, there was an increasing recognition that there was more to women's inequality than mere biology; there were also issues of culture and expectations. The distinction between sex and gender became increasingly important therefore as women's groups campaigned for more opportunities for women. In fact, once contraception became reliable and widespread enabling women to more easily control family size, the focus for the women's movement shifted to the ways in which legislation and education could change their lives. For the next ten years, key campaigns produced new laws for women on the UK statute books. Acts legislating for 'Equal Pay' and 'Anti-discrimination' began to challenge many of the old attitudes of gender and employment. More controversially, the Abortion Act began to chip away at the link between sex and motherhood, and ultimately reinforced the idea that a woman's choice was more important than the sacredness of an embryo.

All this legislation – along with the expansion of the universities and the admission of more women into higher education – meant that the way many women lived would soon be very different from that of their mothers and grandmothers. It offered them far more freedom, choice and independence; it could not, of course, guarantee that they would be more fulfilled.

The present: expectations of women

Our great-grandmothers would probably be surprised at women's lives in Britain today; there have been innumerable changes which have created a very different society for women.

In contrast to previous generations, women, including mothers, are much more involved in public life, especially at a local level. Most women now work outside the home, and this includes mothers of small children – the majority of mothers go back to work after maternity leave. In Britain an estimated 70 per cent of mothers with 9- to 12-month-old babies now do some paid work – compared to only 25 per cent twenty-five years ago. Younger fathers often play a full part in childcare and child-rearing; some may even earn less than their partners, or work at home.

Today, women are also active in almost all the professions. Women's new economic independence – along with the provisions of the Welfare State – has made them much less dependent upon a male partner. This has meant that when a relationship breaks up it has been easier for women to manage financially than before, even though the statistics on child support from absent fathers indicate a reluctance from some divorced men to continue to support their family.

Reliance on the extended family also decreased through the 1990s as relatives are now less likely to live within easy access of each other, and, with increased travel for education or immigration, may well be split across continents. It has been interesting, however, to observe how the increased costs of professional child-care in the first two decades of the twenty-first century have brought some reversal of this. Grandparents now often move to be within easier distance of their children and grandchildren, so that they can be a resource to young working parents.

Receiving a formal education is no longer so strongly influenced by the question of gender. Curiously, girls regularly outstrip boys in exam performance in almost all subjects and are attaining increasingly higher grades. The numbers of men and women at university are almost equal, though not in all subjects as more women study languages and men still predominate in the field of technology. Even though the 'appeal to biology' re-emerges in popular form in most generations, there is a general acceptance in the country that culture, expectations and education play the more significant part in shaping gender and gender differences.

Our great-grandmothers would probably be even more puzzled by women's intimate lives in Britain; compared to their own day, it is far more normal for a woman to be sexually active outside marriage. In fact, a substantial proportion of women never marry but may well have a number of sexual partners during their lifetime. It is neither unusual nor abnormal for women to separate 'being mothers' from 'being wives'. At present, about 15 per cent of mothers who give birth are already living on their own, 25 per cent are cohabiting and 60 per cent are married. Of those children who are born into a family context, many experience family breakup and go on to stay with their mother. Of the 13 million dependent children in the UK in 2009, 63 per cent lived with married parents, 13 per cent with cohabiting parents and 24 per cent with lone parents – of whom almost 90 per cent were mothers.[2] In fact, at the age of sixteen, a third of British children are living apart from their biological father – a figure set to rise further if present trends continue. However, our great-grandmothers might find it hard to be persuaded that cohabitation is an improvement on what they experienced in marriage, even given their restrictions and lack of independence. Sadly, statistics suggest that girls who become pregnant whilst cohabiting are very likely to be on their own with the child before that child is two. That means, in everyday terms, that they face the considerable demands of child-rearing with limited support.

One of the indisputable negative facts is that Britain has the highest level of teenage conception found in Western Europe, although the figures have been on a slight downward trend other than during 2007–2008. Figures for the first half of 2007 showed that conception rates for girls under eighteen stood at 42 out of every 1,000 girls.[3] This is six or seven times higher than that of The Netherlands, for example. For girls in Britain between thirteen and fifteen years, the conception rate was an alarming 8 out of every 1,000. About half of all these pregnancies end in abortion. Of those who keep their babies, the fortunate ones have supportive parents or families to share the care and nurture of their offspring. But there are also many isolated young women, who rely almost exclusively on social services for help.

Over the last few years, studies have also focused on children and what their lives are like now in Britain in the light of all the changes that have affected their upbringing. The findings have not been very encouraging. The *Good Childhood Enquiry* conducted in February, 2009 pointed out that children today seem more depressed and anxious than in previous generations.[4] The researchers reported high levels of bullying, isolation and family breakup, with around 28 per cent of all children whose parents have separated having no contact with their fathers three years following separation. A high percentage of these children did not talk intimately to anyone about their concerns. The report also suggested that mothers are increasingly afraid to let children explore the outside world unsupervised: Whilst approximately 39 per cent of today's adults went out unsupervised before their eleventh birthday, only 17 per cent of these same adults believe today's children should be allowed to go out unsupervised. There was a high level of fear for the safety of children.

Other reports have studied teenage relationships and come up with findings which have surprised even the researchers. One study of teenagers aged thirteen to seventeen, carried out by the NSPCC and the University of Bristol found that 90 per cent of the girls had been in an intimate relationship.[5] One third of the girls had suffered sexual abuse in the relationship, with 17 per cent saying they were forced to have sex. A quarter of the girls reported violence at the hands of their boyfriends, and one in sixteen said they had been raped. The most disturbing feature of all was the disclosure that many of these girls now accepted violence as part of intimacy.

All these problems are the downside of a culture where women have made incredible gains in so many areas, and today know a level of freedom which would have been unimaginable a century ago. What it shows is that, for some women, this 'freedom' is actually paper-thin; they are left facing consequences which a more protective and restrictive culture had fought against. The challenges for real freedom in a context of respect for women remain as pertinent as ever.

We can see how the context of women's lives today present Christian women with much to think and pray about. To live as followers of Christ in our era of change and challenge can be both demanding and perplexing. What kind of life-style should we pursue as women? And what priorities should be given to work and relationships? How can we marry the many commitments and demands on our lives with the giving of crucial time to caring for our families?

To answer some of those questions, we need to consider particular issues and pressure points which arise in women's lives.

Issues that affect most women today

It is not difficult to summarise some of the pressure points in women's lives. They can be related to a whole welter of factors – children, schooling, work, other people, illness, travel and money come high on the list. Knowing how to prioritise time is vital, particularly when a weekly timetable pulls us in so many directions. Sometimes it is hard to avoid overwork or even burnout, when we have to negotiate the often conflicting demands that face us. What is more, demands are made yet more intense when visits to parents involve hours of travel, or when women in middle age find themselves caught up in caring for four generations of their family. Even a simple task like getting the family off to church on a Sunday morning might produce unbelievable tension!

When the needs of family and home are put alongside issues at work or in the neighbourhood, the result can be simply exhausting. In fact, a common cry from many women is that there is little time for oneself. Managing finances in times of change or redundancy, coping with breakup or loss within the family, sometimes even taking on ever-increasing responsibilities can all take their toll. It is not unusual to find women struggling with their own sense of personal identity at times like these.

For women who are Christians there are other considerations also. Being a follower of Christ means that we are called to serve other people, to give and not to count the cost. Yet this is enacted against the backcloth of a culture which espouses self-centredness and encourages everyone to live the life they choose. In such a climate, being counter-cultural – whether in relation to work, family, consumption patterns or values – needs to be a conscious part of the Christian life. But at the same time as we work out how we must live, we must remember we are asked not to judge those who have rejected the values we hold, or embraced a lifestyle which we find problematic. To be non-judgmental is also part of our response to God. Instead, God asks us to try to identify with those who struggle or experience brokenness and to help other people face the future with hope.

In every period of history, women who have been followers of Christ have also tried to be people of grace, and to reach out in all circumstances with God's blessing and love. So it is no less a challenge for Christian women in this era to know their identity in Christ, and to live that out in their relationships and concern for others. It is our hope in writing this book that we might encourage one another to think and pray about the issues that we face in seeking to live biblically faithful lives.

Women across the globe

Who is the 'average' Christian woman?

Even though we recognise there are inequalities between people in our own culture, we often suppose that there is some kind of 'average' woman, who enjoys areas of freedom whilst facing different sorts of difficulties. Women's struggles in Britain are fairly similar to those in any affluent societies – whether they are concerned with hardship or breakdown of relationships – and often we find it hard to see beyond our own culture. Too often, we can, unconsciously, carry about a picture in our minds of the 'average Christian' as being white, possibly middle-class, reasonably educated and getting by. So it is a challenge for us to recognise that for hundreds of thousands of Christian women elsewhere in the globe, their struggles are much more fundamental and suffering is part of daily life.

The average Christian woman in our world today is more likely to be: poor, in need of safe water, without adequate sanitation, the mother of many children and struggling to meet all the responsibilities of looking after a large family whilst she works hard to earn a living.

The average Christian mother is likely to suffer the loss of a baby through malnutrition or disease. The average Christian grandmother may well mourn the death of adult children through sweeping epidemics, especially HIV/AIDS, and face the prospect of bringing up her many grandchildren in her old age. She will also be vulnerable to famine, drought, malaria, schistosomiasis and strings of other tropical illnesses, as well as many epidemics which have been eradicated in the affluent world.

The average Christian woman may live in a society where violence towards women is part of the subtext of the culture, and where it is institutionalised in many different forms and practices. She may have undergone female genital mutilation, been raped by warring soldiers, been taken as a child-bride, suffered domestic violence or be involved in helping other women who are damaged or oppressed by it. She may have faced persecution through war or conflict, and may have suffered the violent death of her husband or children. Living with the effects of violence becomes an endemic part of life for far too many women, even in the twenty-first century.

The average Christian woman across the world enjoys few of our educational opportunities, may well have no access to books or learning resources and possesses little chance of studying beyond primary school. She may never have had even the prospect of becoming literate. Her time will be taken up in basic tasks – travelling to and from the well to draw water, growing crops or keeping goats to feed the family.

The average Christian woman will be paid a meagre sum for her work. If she is a farmer, she will have almost no say in the price paid for her goods. If she grows coffee or chocolate it will quite likely be bought for consumption in the West at rock-bottom prices which may not be enough to pay others to harvest the coffee beans. If she is a labourer, working for one of the transnational corporations, she will be paid whatever they deem to be profitable for them, irrespective of her needs. The selling price of anything she produces will be decided by the global market – by affluent countries who have little concept of a fair wage when the work is done by those who are poor.

The average Christian woman will be particularly vulnerable to environmental hardship, although she will have done little herself to contribute to the problem. Even though most of the carbon dioxide emissions are produced by affluent nations, the poorer countries pay the cost year after year. The United Nations Intergovernmental Panel for Climate Change forecasts an increase in extreme climate problems – floods, droughts, erratic storms – in virtually every corner of the globe.[6] Those already struggling to survive on low lying land, steep slopes, river banks and marshy coastal areas will be the first to feel the effects of the rapid weather changes. Many may well be obliged to become environmental refugees as the land they lived on can no longer sustain them.[7]

From this short summary, it is clear that many women across the globe know little of the security that we enjoy. They face uncertainty and struggle – whether in terms of finance, health, family life, food provision, war or environmental problems. That is one reason why a rich community life is so crucial and why good neighbour and family relations make survival and growth possible. It is often said in Africa that 'it takes a whole village to bring up a child', which indicates that women in particular see the care of the young as the responsibility of all of them. We have much to learn in our affluent cultures about the strength of interdependence and mutual reliance. They have so much to teach us about the commitment we need to give one another. For example, in struggling areas, churches in particular are places where Christian women and men encourage each other, care for the weak, and support widows and orphans. The stories of Christian communities are full of challenge –they know what it means to be the body of Christ together as they combat HIV/AIDS and the effects of violence.

We often describe the Church in some of these countries as the 'suffering Church' where Christians suffer through poverty, persecution, silence and injustice. What is so remarkable is that the suffering Church is often also the growing Church – for it is in these areas of struggle and pain that faithfulness to Christ draws many others into believing and belonging. Some of the most vibrant expressions of Christian faith and love are found in places of acute material and physical need.

Drawing conclusions

When we speak of women and 21st-century culture, we need therefore to recognise how varied and diffuse is the pattern of women's lives and how much each culture across the world needs the empowering hope of the gospel. For, despite the way our cultural differences and geographical distances separate us, we remain women who are called to fellowship with each other. We are to know the bonds of sisterhood and prayer at this time of history, as members of the body of Christ involved in a global network of care and witness. It is surely a demanding calling, but at the very least, any one of us can learn about the lives of others, and pray for one another. We can also take a step beyond, and ask God what we might be doing in our own context and much further afield so that we can share the good news of Christ. When we do, we soon find that it is a wonderful privilege and responsibility to be entrusted with the task of enabling women everywhere to experience more of the freeing and empowering love of God.

Pause to Reflect

What pressure points do you find evident in the women you minister to?

What in this chapter surprised or challenged you?

Turn these thoughts into prayer for women both locally and globally.

NOTES

1. For further details on the history of emigration to Australia see:
   http://www.immi.gov.au/media/fact-sheets/04fifty.htm
   An interesting article about Kylie Minogue's mother who emigrated from Wales is also
   available: http://www.dailymail.co.uk/tvshowbiz/article-1245979
2. Statistics drawn from 'Social Trends 2009' published by TSO – formerly HMSO.
3. Figures taken from 'A Measure of Survival: Calculating Women's Sexual and Reproductive
   Risks', *Population Action International* (Washington: 2007). The World Health Organization also
   publishes a regular *World Health Report* which engages with these issues.
4. Richard and Judy Dunn, *A Good Childhood: Searching for values in a competitive age* (London:
   Children's Society, 2009).
5. Study authored by Christine Barter, Melanie McCarry, David Berridge and Kathy Evans,
   'Partner exploitation and violence in teenage intimate relationships' (University of Bristol
   and NSPCC: September 2009). *The Journal of The Royal College of Obstetricians and Gynaecologists*
   (BJOG) also provides a number of articles on the impact of women's sexuality upon
   contemporary health.
6. *Intergovernmental Panel on Climate Change* from IPCC workshop entitled 'Sea Level Rise and Ice
   Sheet Instabilities', (Kuala Lumpur: June 2010).
7. For further information on the impacts of climate change upon poor people globally and what
   we can do to help, please see: http://www.tearfund.org

PART 2:

Personal Foundations

LIVING THE LIFE
Lynn Penson

Do you ever feel that you should wait until you feel 'good enough' or sufficiently 'holy' before embarking on working with others? For most, if not all of us, such thoughts will result in us never getting started! If we do happen to think that we have 'arrived', I suggest we are either delusional or in heaven. I continue to take great comfort and encouragement from the phrase, 'For when I am weak, then I am strong' (2 Cor. 12:10). This is a good reminder that God can use me best when I feel lacking in my own strength and know that I still have a long way to go.

Nevertheless, and importantly, if we are to lead others we need to be mindful of how we conduct ourselves. In his advice to Timothy, Paul gives warning on the particular responsibility anyone in any form of leadership has in the way they live (1 Tim. 3) As we consider suggestions of some of the characteristics of a good leader, you might want to consider which of these are marks of your character, and which might need a little more work!

Integrity

The highest compliment someone could pay me would be to say I am a woman of integrity. Integrity seems to sum up all that is good and wholesome and honest in a person's character and, for me, incorporates the sense of being godly.

We all have those hidden things that we would prefer others not to know about. We do not need to tell the world everything about ourselves – our thoughts, feelings and actions – but we do need to live our lives in such a way that we are being honest with ourselves and with others.

John Maxwell wrote: 'when I have integrity, my words and my deeds match up. I am who I am, no matter where I am or who I am with.'[1] We live in a world where leaders are constantly being caught out – bankers, politicians, and even, sadly, Church leaders. We want leaders we can trust, those that we can follow with confidence.

When we read about Jesus, we see that He was the same whether with His friends, His followers, His family, religious or political leaders, Roman, Jew, Samaritan. His words and deeds lined up perfectly; there was no pretence or changing sides depending on who He was with. He was truly authentic. Jesus was able to inspire others to follow Him, even when blazing an uncomfortable trail, because His life shone with truth and He led by being genuine. His disciples could respond with confidence when He called them to 'Come, follow me' (see Matt. 4:18–19).

Pause to reflect

Can people have full confidence in you? Do they trust you to practise what you preach? Do they believe you would not expect them to say and do things that you would not say and do yourself? Can they follow your leading and example with full confidence, because you live out what you say?

Being secure

Probably all of us will struggle with being fully secure. It is important that we get on with the task God has given us wherever we are, but it is good to be aware of the extent to which we might find leading or working with others difficult, if we are insecure. Recognising the causes and effects of being insecure can help us to appreciate what it is to be secure. Understanding these causes is the first step to dealing with insecurity.

People who are insecure will often be driven by their need to gain approval from others. This may lead them to be easily swayed by other people's opinions, and to appear contradictory. In their efforts to please people, they may give their time to everyone else's needs without consideration of their own, which might result in burnout or growing resentment over time as their own concerns are subjugated. Dealing with disapproval is extremely difficult for insecure people, so criticism is taken personally and can be quite damaging to relationships.

It is very hard for us when we are working with others, if we are always looking for approval. We need to be able to deal with different opinions, and even handle criticism well, without feeling threatened. Recognising that others will think differently, giving them permission to voice their views and concerns whilst at the same time retaining our views, creates a healthy, mutually respectful atmosphere.

Insecurity can also lead to feeling threatened by others who appear more competent at certain tasks. This creates friction, but may also produce a situation where the leader stifles growth in others out of fear that they might develop beyond the ability of the leader.

In looking at Jesus, we see someone who knew and held to His beliefs and was not swayed by others, even when they were highly regarded religious leaders of the day. He was secure in the love of His Father and was able to stand firm against all opposition, disapproval, and the different opinions of others. He drew other people to Him, but rather than keeping them from developing, trusted them to go out without Him to preach and heal.

A good leader will draw others around her, model good qualities and teach well, but then hold lightly those she is leading, remaining undisturbed by those people forging a path ahead of her. Rather than restricting the vision of those she leads, leaving them ready but with nowhere to go, she will enlarge their vision, equipping and inspiring them, and, in so doing, empower them to reach their potential. There may be a tinge of sadness in feeling left behind, but the joy of seeing someone else soar should more than make up for this.

Pause to reflect

Are you able to work with people without demanding their approval, and with no hint of jealousy? Do people have permission to 'fly higher' than you? Are you aware of empowering rather than disempowering others?

Considered responses

How easy it is to respond to another person's urgent request, leaving to one side what is actually more important. Many family members have been hurt by well-meaning parents or spouses rushing to help someone in need, and putting their own important family commitments to one side. As we work with others, it is vital that we consider what our priorities are and how we will safeguard them. This not only protects us and our family relationships, but also encourages responsibility in those we are helping.

Furthermore, we live in a time of instant communication, and that has caused unhappiness as responses are made immediately without adequate time to give a measured reaction. I have seen difficult relationships become intolerable from reactive text messaging. My father used to say, 'Fools rush in where angels fear to tread,' which is similar to another saying, 'Act in haste, repent at leisure'. Sometimes it is necessary to stop and carefully consider what we are about to say or do.

As women, we are particularly susceptible to emotional outbursts and mood swings at certain times and so it is especially important to think about the possible impact of our words and actions when we are feeling emotionally vulnerable.

When Jesus was with His disciples He told them: 'Do not leave Jerusalem, but wait for the gift my Father promised, which you have heard me speak about' (Acts 1:4).

Notice the word 'wait'. I find waiting a frustrating task; even joining the 'wrong queue' exasperates me. How often have I wanted to 'get on and get it sorted', before I have had a chance to think through what is best. Can you imagine what would have happened if His followers had been anxious to get out and do something rather than wait as Jesus had instructed?

Jesus knew that immediate responses were not always the best. He did not rush to the rescue when Lazarus was taken so ill, and yet the outcome was positive. He stopped to find out who had been healed by touching His cloak, whilst Jairus was no doubt urging Him to get to his sick daughter as quickly as possible.

Pause to reflect

Do you tend to rush to 'rescue' those who shout loudest, whilst neglecting those nearest to you?

Good priorities

I think many ministers wish they had more activists when it comes to filling those ever-increasing church roles. Personally, I like to get out there and be busy with whatever is there to be done, but a lesson that has gone deeply into my spirit is that of 'being', not just 'doing'. For the past two years I have taken a regular Quiet Day. What a battle goes on as I look at my list of jobs to do on my precious day off, but if I make the decision not to take that day out, it leaves me impoverished. To take regular quiet days is something relatively new to my experience, but I know it is invaluable for this season of my life, and I trust it will become part of my way of life for many years. It comes from a need to be deeply rooted in the things of God, and to be drawing from Him in order to be able to give to others.

Jesus had three years, once he had begun His ministry, to accomplish what He had been sent to do. Whilst a great deal was packed into those few years, nevertheless we note those times He took himself away from the crowds and even away from His closest followers, to be by Himself, to be with His Father.

Following breakfast on the beach after His resurrection, Jesus asks Simon Peter the question, 'Simon son of John, do you truly love me more than these?' (John 21:15).

Various suggestions have been offered for what 'these' entails, but whatever the comparison is about, it is a question of priorities – who do you love most of all? What or who is your priority when it comes to your devotion?

Pause to reflect

How easy do you find it to stop and be with God, to listen to Him rather than talk at Him? What is your answer to the questions: Who do you love most of all? What or who is your priority when it comes to your devotion?

Healthy balance

God's creative plan for us was to include both work and rest as part of our rhythm of life. We need to heed the Designer's instructions: 'Six days you shall labour and do all your work, but the seventh day is a Sabbath to the LORD your God. On it you shall not do any work...'(Exod. 20:9–10) If we work full-time and then spend Sunday 'working' within our church, we should ensure that we take time off to rest and refresh ourselves on another day of the week. Jesus reminded us that the Sabbath was made for human beings, not human beings for the Sabbath (Mark 2:27), making it clear that this is not about a legalistic approach to time off. Some jobs or roles require people to work outside of the usual pattern, but the important thing is to ensure those patterns of rest are built in.

Some people will be driven to prove themselves through being busy. Women who are leaders can so easily fall into this trap, and those looking to their lead might feel the need to emulate their hectic lifestyle. However, leaders can, and should, be role models for healthy patterns of living.

Equally important is that we don't neglect work, but that we put our efforts into it – as Paul reminds his readers, 'Whatever you do, work at it with all your heart, as working for the Lord, not for men' (Col. 3:23).

I believe that we can contribute a great deal to our own lives and those of others when we live a balanced lifestyle of work, rest and play (as the advert for the chocolate bar used to suggest), in accordance with the Maker's design.

In Matthew's Gospel we read a parable about ten bridesmaids (Matt. 25:1–13). They were to wait for the bridegroom, but were so tired that they fell asleep, only to be woken by his arrival at midnight. To their dismay, five of the young women discovered their oil had run out whilst the lamps of the other five continued to burn brightly. Even in those times of rest, we can be ready for what is to come next as we wait for God's timing.

Pause to reflect

Do you have a good work, rest and play balance in your life? Are there any of these that need adjusting?

Compassion

Jesus is often described as having done something for people out of His sense of compassion:

'When he saw the crowds, he had *compassion* on them, because they were harassed and helpless, like sheep without a shepherd' (Matt. 9:36, my italics).
'... he had *compassion* on them and healed their sick' (Matt. 14:14, my italics).
'Jesus called his disciples to him and said, I have *compassion* for these people; they have already been with me three days and have nothing to eat. I do not want to send them away hungry, or they may collapse on the way' (Matt. 15:32, my italics).

The Gospels paint a beautiful picture of Jesus relating to people of every class and background with such kindness and generosity, and drawing them to Him. Do you know people like that among your acquaintances? They are people who have a genuine thoughtfulness in how they relate, and that is accompanied by a gentle and peaceful spirit. They extend friendship; not insisting, always inviting. They give without an agenda, without looking for something in return – not even friendship. These are people who are not usually counted as leaders in today's society. However, if Jesus is counted as a leader, they must be ranking highly with such qualities. This is a quality of servant leadership; leading with the aim of serving others rather than serving self.

There are many other qualities that are important – patience, perseverance, empathy, ability to listen well. The list is endless and daunting.

As we look to Jesus as our role model, we can see character qualities that we know bring out the very best in ourselves, the best in others, and produce transformation in relationships.

Pause to reflect

As you consider people who may possess such virtues, consider your own character in light of the qualities outlined above.

Take some time to consider your positive qualities. What and who has helped to shape them in you? How can you use these to help others?

What one quality would you like to develop? As you pray for the help of the Holy Spirit, find ways to practise this quality.[2]

NOTES
1. John Maxwell, *Developing the Leader Within You* (Georgia: Injoy Inc., 2005) p.35.
2. I have found *The Fourfold Leadership of Jesus* by Andrew Watson (Abingdon: BRF, 2008) very useful in exploring this topic, and have drawn on his material.

Discovering Your Basic Spiritual Gift

Jeannette Barwick

Every Christian has at least one spiritual gift. Discovering what your gift or gifts are can become a turning point for you, as the process sets you free to minister with confidence and joy. Joy comes as you exercise your gifts.

Some years ago I discovered what my spiritual gifts are. Being able to identify them helped me greatly, and since then has influenced the way I have contributed to the ministry of CWR at Waverley Abbey House, to my church, and beyond. I used the exercise on page 68 which was developed by Selwyn Hughes many years ago to help the people in his pastoral care to discover their spiritual gifts.[1]

What are spiritual gifts?

Spiritual gifts should be distinguished from human talents which can operate without divine assistance. Moreover, spiritual gifts should be distinguished from spiritual fruits. The fruit of the Spirit describe moral virtues (Gal. 5:22–23), while spiritual gifts relate to abilities that equip Christians for service.

In 1 Peter 4:10 we read: 'As each one has received a gift, minister it to one another, as good stewards of the manifold grace of

---

1. Some churches find it helpful to use the basic gift chart. 'Discovering Your Basic Gift' is a free download from the CWR website – see www.cwr.org.uk/free-downloads

God' (NKJV). We have gifts; they are given to us for others that God by His Spirit might flow through us, bringing His living water to the weary and thirsty world. The New Testament introduces us to three distinct streams of gifts which are listed respectively in Romans 12:6–8, 1 Corinthians 12:8–10 and Ephesians 4:11–12.

The first group, in Romans, are basic life purpose and motivation gifts for the individual. Those in the second group are given to benefit or strengthen the Body of Christ, and those in the third group are given to facilitate and equip the Church.

God builds into our personalities at the moment of conception certain aptitudes and abilities which later, through growth and development, become observable. Once we become Christians, however, a spiritual transformation takes place in which the Holy Spirit regenerates our human spirits and brings us new life and a new identity. There takes place within us, whether we feel it or not, an inner thrust, a distinct motivation which leads us towards a specific form of ministry in the Body of Christ. This inner drive is what constitutes a basic gift as listed in Romans 12.

Precisely stated, a spiritual gift is a divine, supernatural ability, given by God to enable a Christian to serve and to minister. More simply put, a spiritual gift is a special tool for ministry.

Points to ponder

I hope the exercise on page 68 helps you not only to see yourself more clearly, but also to see the people in your church in a new way.

1. When you consider that Paul's listing of the seven basic gifts in Romans 12 follows on from his earnest appeal 'to offer your bodies as living sacrifices', it suggests that we ought to approach the whole subject in an attitude of prayerful expectancy. Dedication must precede revelation. So, spend some time with God in quiet prayer and meditation, asking Him to help you find and develop your unique ministry.
2. Remember that God's gifts are often in line with a natural ability, and this is why our natural faculties may point to the direction in which a spiritual gift may be used.

3. The absence of any particular gift does not excuse us from obedience to other scriptural commands. If a person does not feel they have a gift of 'giving', they are still expected to support the Lord's work financially. Similarly, if a Christian does not possess the gift of 'mercy', they are still expected to 'help the weak [and] be patient with everyone' (1 Thess. 5:14). This may raise the question: 'If we are all expected to do so much, where is the need for specific gifts?' In some ways the Church is like a football team in which, although the players each have a separate function, all are expected to try to score a goal. Each one of us has a responsibility to work for Christ, but the major part of our work must be along the line of the spiritual gift (or gifts) which we have been given.

4. Confirmation that you have a certain basic gift will also come through the discernment of other believers. In fact, other Christians may see a gift in you long before you yourself are aware of it. It helps to prayerfully share with other Christians your conclusions before attempting to develop your gifts.

5. Just as a deep, settled peace pervades our being when we are in the centre of God's will, so a feeling of great joy arises when exercising a basic gift. This inner joy can be a clue to the presence of a gift, and this is often unconsciously communicated to those on the receiving end of your ministry.

6. Once you discover you have a basic gift, don't go around telling everyone, but adopt the attitude described by Paul in Philippians 2:3–4: 'Don't be selfish; don't live to make a good impression on others. Be humble, thinking of others as better than yourself. Don't just think about your own affairs, but be interested in others, too, and in what they are doing' (TLB). Watch for opportunities to minister using your basic spiritual abilities, and be quick to act upon what God is showing you.

It has been said that when we are operating in our gifts we experience maximum effectiveness with minimum weariness, as opposed to minimum effectiveness with maximum weariness when we are involved in areas that do not use our gifts. However, if you find you are involved in a responsibility you think is outside your gifting pray about it carefully. God may well want you to continue for a season.

All God's children have gifts

1. I enjoy presenting God's truth in an inspired and enthusiastic way.

2. I am always ready to overlook my own personal comfort in order that the needs of others may be met.

3. I find great delight in explaining the truth of a text within its context.

4. I am able to verbally encourage those who waver and are spiritually troubled.

5. I am able to manage my financial affairs efficiently so that I can give generously to the Lord's work.

6. I find it easy to delegate responsibility and organise others towards spiritual achievement.

7. I readily find myself sympathising with the misfortune of others.

8. I am conscious of a persuasiveness of speech when encouraging people to examine their spiritual motives.

9. I have the knack of making people feel at home.

10. I delight in digging out facts concerning the Bible so that I can pass them on to others.

11. I have a deep concern to encourage people toward spiritual growth and achievement.

12. I am cheerful about giving material assets so that the Lord's work can be furthered.

13. I am able to effectively supervise the activities of others.

14. I enjoy visiting those in hospital, or those confined to their homes due to illness or disability.

15. I am able to present the Word of God to a congregation of people with clarity and conviction.

16. I am happy when asked to assist others in the Lord's work.

17. I am concerned that truth should be presented in a clear fashion with proper attention to the meaning of words.

18. I am at my best when treating those who are spiritually wounded.

19. I have no problem in joyfully entrusting my assets to others for the work of the ministry.

20. I am able to plan the actions of others with ease and supply them with details which will enable them to work efficiently.

21. I have great concern for those involved in trouble.

22. I find myself preaching for a verdict whenever I present the truths of the Word of God.

23. I delight in providing a gracious haven for guests.

24. I am diligent in my study of the Bible and give careful attention to necessary research.

25. I am able to help those who need counselling over personal problems.

26. I am concerned over the question of financial assistance being available for all sections of the church.

27. I am deeply sensitive to the need of a smooth running administration so that every phase of activity is carried out decently and in order.

28. I work happily with those who are ignored by the majority.

29. I find my preaching brings people to a definite point of decision.

30. I enjoy taking the load from key people so that they can put more effort into their own particular task.

31. I am able to explain well how the Bible hangs together.

32. I am acutely aware of the things that hold people back in their spiritual development and long to help them overcome their problems.

33. I am careful with money and continually pray over its proper distribution in the work of the Lord.

34. I know where I am going and am able to take others with me.

35. I am able to relate to others emotionally and am quick to help when help is needed.

Instructions

Alongside are 35 statements which may help you to discover your basic gift or gifts. Rate yourself with the following scale by writing the appropriate number in the corresponding number square in the grid below. Ask yourself: 'Is this statement true in my spiritual life and experience?' Indicate your score in the appropriate number square using the following scale.

| Greatly 3 | Some 2 | Little 1 | Not at all 0 |

After you have completed rating yourself for each of the 35 statements, add the scores in each horizontal row. Record the number in the Total column. Your total score for each row indicates your level of interest in that particular gift. The highest scores may lead you to a clearer understanding of the basic spiritual gift or gifts which God has deposited in your life.

A chart to help you find and develop your unique ministry

(fill in total and gift after completing your score)

Row A	1.	8.	15.	22.	29.	Total	Gift
Row B	2.	9.	16.	23.	30.		
Row C	3.	10.	17.	24.	31.		
Row D	4.	11.	18.	25.	32.		
Row E	5.	12.	19.	26.	33.		
Row F	6.	13.	20.	27.	34.		
Row G	7.	14.	21.	28.	35.		

Key to your spiritual gift

Row A–Prophecy;   Row E–Giving;

Row B–Serving;   Row F–Leading or Co-ordinating;

Row C–Teaching;   Row G–Empathy or Mercy

Row D–Stimulating the faith of others;

Once you have discovered your basic gift – what next? Ask God to flood your life with His Holy Spirit so that you will become inwardly sensitive to the best gifts to expand and amplify your ministry. These gifts of the Spirit are described and defined in 1 Corinthians 12. If God, in His sovereignty, has ordained you to function in the role of an apostle, prophet, pastor, teacher or evangelist then this will become apparent to you through the recognition of those of your own local church, and by a spiritual witness to your own heart. Don't be overconcerned with aiming at being an apostle, prophet, pastor, teacher or evangelist. Concentrate on the depth of your ministry, and God will concentrate on the breadth.

Definition	Explanation	Dangers
Gifts of God		
1. Prophecy – or the God-given ability to present truth.	A persuasiveness and power in speech which brings to light things previously concealed.	a. Proud of rhetoric or persuasive speech. b. Dependent on ability to speak rather than on the Holy Spirit to convict. c. Seeing people as groups – not individuals. d. Judgmental and a sharp tongue without love.
2. Serving or demonstrating love by meeting practical needs so that others can be free for service.	An ability to detect personal needs; to overlook personal comfort so that the needs of others can be met (Rom. 12:10).	a. Proud of good deeds. b. Pushy or premature in attempting to meet the needs of others before they themselves realise what those needs are. c. Bitter when good deeds are not appreciated. d. Over emphasis on practical – neglect of spiritual.
3. Teaching or clarifying truth by ensuring the accuracy of context etc.	An ability to research and unearth facts from Scripture (Rom. 12:12). This involves diligence, fervency in study and careful research.	a. Boasting of knowledge one has accumulated. b. Concentration on details rather than principles. c. Captivated by research rather than responses. d. Believing truth is discerned through intellect.
4. Stimulating the faith of others in specific action towards definite goals.	An ability to counsel others and encourage them toward spiritual growth (Rom. 12:12).	a. Boasting about personal results. b. Discouraged when progress is slow. c. Indiscretion in sharing results. d. Giving too much time to the wrong people.
5. Giving or joyfully entrusting personal assets or possessions to others for the work of the ministry.	An ability to organise personal business; able to wisely invest and make quick and sound decisions about the right use of money.	a. Becoming proud of one's generosity. b. Measuring spiritual success by material gain. c. Attempting to buy influence with money. d. Overlooking long-range goals.
6. Leading or co-ordinating the activities of others for the achievement of a common goal.	An ability to preside or lead; seeing future consequences of one's actions; able to distinguish major objectives and help others visualise them.	a. Proud of power over people. b. Using people to accomplish goals. c. Overlooking character faults in those who can be useful to reaching goals.
7. Empathising by an ability to identify with and comfort those in distress.	An ability to sympathise deeply with the misfortunes of others, mentally and emotionally relating and giving aid.	a. Proud of ability to sympathise. b. Resenting others who are not sympathetic to needs. c. Failing to be firm – guided by emotions, not logic.
Gifts of the Holy Spirit		
1. *Tongues* – the ability to speak supernaturally in a language never learned.	Used in (a) congregational worship to bring a message from God or (b) privately as a devotional exercise.	a. Regarding 'tongues' as a mark of maturity. b. Proud of the prominence the gift inevitably brings.

Gift	Used to...	Cautions
2. *Interpretation of Tongues* – the ability to supernaturally interpret a message given in tongues.	Used to interpret the mind of the Spirit as given through a message in other tongues.	**a.** Dependency on initiative. **b.** Over zealousness in failing to develop sensitivity.
3. *Prophecy* – the ability to supernaturally convey God's message for the moment in the language of speaker and hearers.	Used to convey a message of edification, exhortation or comfort to God's people at specific times.	**a.** Expressing personal feelings within the prophecy. **b.** Extending the ministry beyond limits. (Judgmental and harsh.)
4. *Word of Knowledge* – a supernatural revelation to meet an emergency or crisis.	Used to supernaturally impart to a person or group a fact of knowledge which at that moment is otherwise unknown.	**a.** Hesitancy in communicating due to no logical explanation. **b.** Failure to exercise reason.
5. *Word of Wisdom* – a supernatural revelation showing how to apply the right solution.	Used to supernaturally impart to someone the right procedure to take in a difficult situation.	**a.** Overdependency on gifts. **b.** Lack of prayer and spiritual exercise.
6. *Faith* – the supernatural ability to visualise and witness spiritual achievement.	Used to supernaturally empower a person to 'believe' beyond their own natural faith.	**a.** Fear of being proved wrong. **b.** Ignoring others' feelings.
7. *Discerning of spirits* – supernatural ability to discern the source of supernatural manifestations.	Used to detect the presence of evil spirits or to examine the source of manifestation which is dubious.	**a.** Seeing the problem not the person. **b.** Acting harshly – not firmly.
8. *Gifts of Healing* – supernatural ability to bring God's healing power to the sick.	Used to bring deliverance to those bound in disease, infirmity, affliction etc.	**a.** Moving on one's own initiative. **b.** Failure to develop sensitivity.
9. *Working of Miracles* – supernatural ability to suspend natural laws.	Used to bring God's power to bear upon a situation where natural means fail.	**a.** Pride in experience. **b.** Lack of prayer and devotion.

Gifts of Christ

Gift	Used to...	Cautions
1. *Apostle* – the gift of pioneering new territory for the gospel of Christ (example – a modern missionary)	This is a person in whom the gift of Christ dwells for the express purpose of making major inroads with the gospel message.	**a.** Holding attention by virtue of one's position. **b.** Being proud because of personal selection.
2. *Prophet* – the gift of directing vision toward matters of vital concern in relation to immediate goals.	This is a person in whom the gift of Christ dwells for the purpose of elevating spiritual vision in the Body of Christ.	**a.** Attempting to move people by demand rather than love.
3. *Evangelist* – the gift of being able to point men and women to a saving knowledge of the Lord Jesus Christ.	This is a person in whom the gift of Christ dwells for the purpose of attracting large numbers of people to salvation in Christ.	**a.** Failure to recognise other related ministries. **b.** Relinquishing concern once converts have made a decision.
4. *Pastor* – the gift of being a shepherd to the flock of God.	This is a person in whom the gift of Christ dwells for the purpose of developing a group of believers into spiritual maturity.	**a.** Seeing only the needs of the local fellowship. **b.** Attempting to meet every need by personal effort.
5. *Teacher* – the gift of being able to expound the truths of God's Word in context and to make profound truths simple.	This is a person in whom the gift of Christ dwells for the purpose of edifying the Body of Christ in relation to the basic concepts of successful Christian living.	**a.** Expounding truth without applying principles. **b.** Becoming more interested in principles than people.

MISSION, VISION AND GOALS

Rosalyn Derges

Long before Jesus came as a man to earth, His plan and purpose was set in the heart of God. As He stood in the synagogue in His home town of Nazareth, He proclaimed these words: 'The Spirit of the Lord is on me, because he has anointed me to preach good news to the poor. He has sent me to proclaim freedom for the prisoners and recovery of sight for the blind, to release the oppressed, to proclaim the year of the Lord's favour' (Luke 4:18–19). With firm conviction, as all eyes were on Him, He then declared: 'Today this scripture is fulfilled in your hearing' (Luke 4:21).

What confidence! What certainty! How I long to have the assurance of the purpose and plan for my life. Then I look a little closer and see that in actual fact, Jesus' life was lived in a very practical way, and I can observe how He achieved his mission. He made His life accessible to those around Him and to me, and by reading the Gospels I begin to understand and experience the pleasure of being invited into Jesus' world.

What I see is that He lived on purpose, from gathering His disciples to healing the sick, from teaching the thousands to meeting the ones and twos; He took every opportunity to use all of heaven's resources to bring life into every situation. Jesus made the kind of choices I can make – the most important being the time He spent with God. He was perfectly in tune with His Father, and perfectly at ease within Himself. He did what He saw the Father doing (John 5:17,19–20). This was a source of strength, empowerment and direction. It was from this place that He could fulfil His mission and set His vision and goals. As we read, we can observe His relationship with His friends, which reveal so much truth. His conversations with the disciples and others spark off some amazing life teaching. It shows us how imperfect people can be used to fulfil God's plans and purposes. This continues to give me hope. As He spent time with them, He was effectively empowering them with Himself. I began to see that if I choose to spend time with Him and allow His words and actions to penetrate my heart, I too can be empowered.

Jesus used His gifts publicly to demonstrate visible signs of God's power, as well as privately bringing comfort quietly, almost unseen. He encouraged individuals and taught thousands through parables. His hands were used to create things out of wood and to bring new life to dead bodies. He filled fisherman's nets, and He filled hungry souls. His mission was clear, and He accomplished it in a variety of ways. This shows me that as long as I can understand my purpose, I can find different ways of living it out in my everyday life. Suddenly, I begin to believe that it is possible to live life *on* purpose *for* a purpose, and that purpose is God's plan for my life.

Pause to reflect

Spend some time thanking God for His purposes in your life, and in the lives of those you seek to minister to.

God has a purpose for our life

'Exhibit God with your uniqueness.'[1]

As Christian women, we have invited the power of God to be present in our lives, therefore God's story dovetails into ours. We are made in His image, and so will display some of His attributes. When we have discovered our purpose, how amazing to know that the power of God's Holy Spirit can enable us to achieve that purpose and that we reflect something of who God is. Max Lucado said, 'He custom designed you for a one of a kind assignment.'[2]

How wonderful to imagine that our lives can 'exhibit God'.

In his letter to the Philippians, Paul wrote that he had a strong desire to live fully for Jesus, and that his goal was to 'press on to take hold of that for which Christ Jesus took hold of me' (Phil. 3:12). God has taken hold of all of us for something; we need to tune in to what that is! I believe this is part of the abundant life Jesus promised, that when we are truly living in a place for which we have been created, we experience fullness of joy. God's vision for our lives is to bring Him glory; so whatever our purpose, whatever we do, ultimately it is about bringing praise to God. God knows what He is doing, everything originates with Him; you, your gifts, your potential, everything you are, is for the praise of His glory. The incredible thing is that like Jesus, the plan for our lives was prepared in advance: 'For we are God's workmanship, created in Christ Jesus to do good works, which God prepared in advance for us to do' (Eph. 2:10).

Live on purpose

'His divine power has given us everything we need for life and godliness through our knowledge of him who called us by his own glory and goodness' (2 Pet. 1:3). Here we are told we have everything we need. It is *His* enabling, *His* power, in fact it is Christ in us that gives us everything we need. Being aware that God has got hold of us for something should focus our thinking and behaviour towards that purpose. If we have a sense of uncertainty or confusion, it might be because we have not really given time to consider what our purpose is. Also, there are times when we are busy trying to accomplish goals that were never meant to be ours in the first place. There have been stages in my life where I have wanted to 'batten down the hatches' and run away because I feel I'm on the treadmill of life and want to get off and hide. Anxiety and stress have the potential to send me away from all of the real purpose of my life; being still and reflecting will lead me away from the distractions and into that real purpose.

We need to recognise that in life we are responsible for making choices. When it comes to purpose, we can be deliberate in making those choices. Knowing this and practising it can be very liberating for us in how we make decisions about the use of time. It enables us to prioritise and focus, establishing boundaries so we can begin to get a sense of God's purpose for us, and therefore peace. So, what do we need to prioritise?

Pause to reflect

'We are busy trying to accomplish goals that were never meant to be ours in the first place.' Does this currently apply to you, or someone you are ministering to?

Spend time with God

How many times have we heard the call to 'Be still, and know that I am God' (Psa. 46:10)?

God longs for our ear so He can lead us into all He has. Quite often we don't realise what the possibilities are because we don't spend the time that will fuel those possibilities. God will give us the desires of our hearts. He will put dreams and visions in us that *with Him* we can accomplish. It is crucial, as we fulfil our purpose, to go to the One who has created us for that purpose. As we know, this is what Jesus did. Jesus saw what the Father was doing, and we can too. Eugene Peterson encourages us to get in on what God is doing. He puts it this way: 'What has God been doing here? What traces of grace can I discern in this life? What history of love can I read in this group? What has God set in motion that I can get in on?'[3] And then he encourages us to pray with our eyes open, that is, with awareness. This enables us to take the opportunities that God presents to us in our everyday lives and in our relationships. Jesus modelled this for us with the woman at the well (John 4). It fitted in well with his mission of healing the broken-hearted and setting captives free.

How can we identify our mission?

Dr Martin Luther King Jr said, 'Everyone has the power for greatness – not for fame but greatness, because greatness is determined by service.' We all have the capacity to serve others in some measure, and Dr King links serving to greatness. For many of us, if we can grasp that to identify and live out our purpose means that it will enhance the lives of the people around us, we will gladly try to get hold of it. God has equipped us with personalities and gifts that He knows we can use in that service which will bless others and bring Him glory. This means that whatever those 'works' are, we will have the capacity to fulfil them. The wonderful thing is that our mission in life will most certainly bring us joy because it brings God joy. So how do we know what it is?

When John Maxwell, author, conference speaker and business life-coach was asked at a lecture at the Abundant Life Church in Bradford, 'What's the secret of your passion?', his reply was confident and assured: 'I am gifted at what I do, what I do makes a difference and when I do what I was made to do I feel most alive.' If we take hold of this model we will see that we need to:

a) Be aware of what we are good at – know our gifts
b) Recognise where we make a difference – what benefits others
c) Connect when we feel a sense of satisfaction and achievement

When we align ourselves with our God-given purpose, we will automatically serve others as well as feel and know we're living on purpose. Purpose is one of the foundations God has given us to stand on – it is crucial to our sense of well-being. It will be helpful to focus on what our purpose is and, if possible, to define it so we are clear. Focusing can direct us on the right path and enable us to bring clarity to the paths we don't need to take. In other words, when to say 'Yes' and when to say 'No'.

Mission statement

Our mission will be our life purpose. We saw Jesus' mission statement in Luke 4. The mission statement for our own lives will embrace our reason for being here. It will consist of the big picture for our life and what that life will accomplish. It is not a list of things to achieve, but rather encompasses who we are.

As I was growing up, among the few toys I had were a very precious teddy and a doll. I would sit them down almost every day with pencils and paper and teach them. Although at the age of five I have no idea what knowledge I could have been passing on, I knew in my heart that I wanted to be a teacher. I achieved my goal and became a primary school class teacher, which was to be my career for almost thirty years. I taught in many different schools where I had to adapt to the many different philosophies of education, but I recognised that what motivated me never changed. I longed to encourage each child to reach their potential in whatever way they could, whether intellectual, relational, physical or emotional. Their growth and sense of satisfaction was of paramount importance to me. What I did was to teach; why I did it was related to who I am. I was motivated by a gift of encouragement (Rom. 12:6–8).

Max Lucado says, 'God never called you to be anyone other than you. But he does call you to be the best you you can be. The big question is, at your best, who are you?' In *Cure for the Common Life*, he urges us to find our 'sweet spot', where we are using our strengths and passions to find our optimum place for living the abundant life. When I realised that my sweet spot included encouraging children in this way, and subsequently women in my current ministry, then I had found my overall purpose and therefore could specify my mission statement. It is concise, involves the big picture for my life, and helps me to check out how I'm doing. Therefore my simple statement is 'My purpose is to inspire and encourage others'. I knew I needed to develop this, and as I reflected on my story so far, the thrust of my purpose was to encourage others to find satisfaction in being who they are, using their gifts and abilities. Having trained in CWR's counselling model, I knew that the only way to find this was standing on the foundations of God's love where we find security, self-worth and significance. So my statement became 'To inspire and encourage others to be who they are by reaching out to touch and be touched by God's love'. 1 Thessalonians 2:11–12 says, 'For you know that we dealt with each of you as a father deals with his own children, encouraging, comforting and urging you to live lives worthy of God, who calls you into his kingdom and glory.' This has become my 'life-verse'.

Pause to reflect

What do I love to do? When do I feel a real sense of purpose and satisfaction? What gifts do I have? How does this fit into God's picture/story? Create a mission statement and gradually develop it.

The focus of a vision

Having a vision breathes life into our purpose. It brings clarity and enables us to have a focus. While we have abilities and talents and can identify our life mission, we need to enhance it and release it by being deliberate and developing it into all it can be.

I might know what my purpose is, but if I lack passion and initiative I might never get it off the ground. Jesus spent time with His friends discussing issues, and they sparked one another into action. Spending time with people who encourage and challenge us can be a real gift. It is often here that we are provoked into fulfilling part of our calling. Preparation, too, is a key, as it can enhance what is natural, as does practice for a singer or musician. Jesus prepared by spending time with the Father. We can look for ways to grow and develop our skills through training, for example. Vision enables us to know how our mission is going to be fulfilled – we need to be able to *see* it.

My particular mission statement could take me into all sorts of avenues, and I could find myself in meltdown. So how do I define the vision?

In an article called 'Good to Great', author Jim Collins said 'The real path to greatness, it turns out, requires simplicity and diligence. It requires clarity, not instant illumination. It demands each of us to focus on what is vital – and to eliminate all the extraneous distractions.'[4]

It was probably time to 'eliminate all the extraneous distractions'! I had become aware that God was moving me on from my beloved career. I had been praying for an opportunity to reflect on my future and found myself in hospital with a need for a hysterectomy. It gave me three months of clear time to pray and seek God for the way ahead. The vision part of my life, my particular focus, was going to change from children to women. I felt ill-equipped in many ways. What had I to offer? I would feel so inadequate. Training would help with this, but I also had to take the opportunity to develop a women's ministry, which I began to do in our home. And so began a whole new chapter in my life and the lives of others that has grown over the last ten years. What a joy to connect with God's vision for your life and go with what He is inviting you to do.

Vision statement

'Your vision statement adds the all-important how. It defines the distinctive and specific ways that you will accomplish your mission.'[5] We need specific strategies. How do we fulfil our mission – what are we going to *do*?

This will depend on our talents, passions, personality, skills and experience. My particular vision has changed over time as I have gained experience and confidence. So my vision statement has developed accordingly – reflecting my gifts and calling. Years ago, a friend came with me into a Sunday school class, as I needed extra help. She gave me feedback afterwards saying that it was as if a light were switched on when I got up to talk to the children. I loved what I did! It was a safe place for me; working with women was not necessarily a safe place – my confidence was not as robust. The development of self-belief because of the knowledge that God has equipped me gave me the confidence to have a go and 'do it afraid'. It can be difficult to move on; there are times we hold on to what we have always done because it is familiar. But our fruit-bearing is seasonal.

Our mission statement might be the same as thousands of others – but as we define it by our vision, it becomes more specific. We need to find the unique ways in which we accomplish our purpose. Think of it as a compass keeping us in the right direction and enabling us to measure our progress and establish priorities. What will enable you to accomplish your mission? What do you love to do? What are you good at? I sing and lead worship; it is a delight to me. If I see it as a way in which I can fulfil my mission, somehow it enhances how I do it. So the mission plus vision can be seen as this: 'My purpose is to encourage others to be who they are by reaching out to touch and be touched by God's love. I will do this by leading worship, preparing and teaching, getting alongside and creating opportunities for people to explore relationship with God for themselves.'

Pause to reflect

What could your vision be? Discuss with those you trust how you might pursue your personal mission/purpose. Write down some ideas in pictures/diagrams/Post-it notes.

Goals

It might help to think of a goal as a specific aim you have in mind for a particular purpose. In the women's group I lead, there are specific goals in terms of what subjects we are going to explore, and my goal might be to bring teaching, encourage discussion and create opportunities for development in that area until we feel it is time to move on. From a personal perspective, my specific goals prevent me from experiencing 'roller coaster' living!

I'm a list person. It is very important for me to create lists and tick them off as I go along. And, yes, if I do something over and above my list, I add it and then tick it off. Generally those lists prohibit me from doing too much. They also help me to avoid the insecurity of knowing what to do next. Years of long summer holidays saw me looking back on those six weeks wondering what I did with the time. Currently, I enjoy the freedom of creating my own working day, and I also enjoy the feeling of knowing I have used my time well. However, when I have achieved my goals, I have the pleasure of allowing myself the freedom that accomplishing the task gives me, and I curl up with a good book or film or, if there is enough energy, sharing relationship.

'The purpose of goals is to focus your attention and give you direction, not to identify a final destination.'[6] With goals, it helps if they are clear, able to be resourced and checked if they are going to be fruitful. For example, beginning a praying group for parents is a clear goal. The next question is, who is going to run it and where? It could be done by you or someone who has an interest, in a home or homes. Finally we need to check it fits into our vision and purpose, and if so, we might need to make adjustments to time and availability as well as being aware of differences it could make to others, both positive and negative.

The goal of this chapter is to enable you and me to assess what we are each doing with our lives. Evaluating where we are, what we are doing, how we are doing it, and if we still feel we are moving in God's purpose for our lives can be really helpful. Here is a check-up on LIFE:

- L – Love to do (Am I really doing what I love and am gifted to do?)
- I – Invest in and Involve others (Is what I'm doing making a difference?)
- F – Focus and Fuel (Am I experiencing personal growth and development?)
- E – Evaluate (Again!)

> Do you not know? Have you not heard? The LORD is the everlasting God, the Creator of the ends of the earth. He will not grow tired or weary, and his understanding no one can fathom. He gives strength to the weary and increases the power of the weak. Even youths grow tired and weary, and young men stumble and fall; but those who hope in the LORD will renew their strength. They will soar on wings like eagles; they will run and not grow weary, they will walk and not be faint. (Isa. 40:28–31)

NOTES
1. Max Lucado, *Cure for the Common Life* (Nashville, TN: Thomas Nelson, 2006).
2. Ibid.
3. Eugene H. Peterson, *The Contemplative Pastor* (Grand Rapids: William B. Eerdmans Publishing Co., 1993).
4. Jim Collins, 'Good to Great', www.jimcollins.com/article_topics/articles/good-to-great.html
5. Judy Rushfeldt, www.lifetoolsforwomen.com
6. John Maxwell, *Thinking for a Change* (Nashville, TN: FaithWords, 2003).

LISTENING TO GOD

Rosalyn Derges

Call to me and I will answer you and tell you great and unsearchable things you do not know. (Jeremiah 33:3)

As soon as I pray, you answer me; you encourage me by giving me strength. (Psalm 138:3, NLT)

Communication

Who's doing all the talking? When I was a teenager I wrote a song called 'Two-way Communication'.

> Two-way communication with my Lord
> Two-way conversation word by word.
> Telling Him I love Him
> Telling me He loves me
> Special moments sharing
> Moments filled with love.

These are simple sentiments, yet when I wrote it, I was experiencing a real sense of God's presence in my life. It was a presence that required a commitment *from* me as I knew God had made a commitment *to* me.

Our prayer life can consist of a need to pour out our hearts to God, where we share our pain and our joys. In prayer we are able to worship God by telling Him how great He is, and indeed we are made for worship and to do this is essential for us as His daughters. We come to God with requests and petitions for others, as well as personal needs. And we come to God at times when we long to hear His voice speaking into our hearts for guidance, for encouragement, to experience renewal and to know that we are loved and cherished. But how often do we truly wait to hear that voice which brings such satisfaction to the depths of our heart and spirit?

Patsy Clairmont said:

> Usually when we pray, we know exactly what we want God to do. We've given our situation much thought, we've checked out the pros and cons, considered our options, and decided how God should work. As we kneel in prayer, we unfold carefully laid out plans, hoping for His stamp of approval. Once we get the nod from on high, we can move forward smoothly with life.[1]

How many of us have experienced that, I wonder?

God has created us for relationship, and relationship requires communication. Are we demanding in our need for answers, expecting to find out what we need to know immediately? We can find it hard to wait for an answer; we like instant responses. But in order to hear what is on someone's heart we have to hear what they have to say, and with God the answers can sometimes come slowly.

Pause to reflect

What is my prayer life like? Do I do most of the talking? Do I expect quick answers?

Whose voice am I listening to?

There are so many voices that clamour for our attention. Depending on what stage of life we are at, these voices can belong to friends, family, colleagues, magazine articles, as well as advertisements and photographs of impossibly slim women. The loudness of these voices can sometimes create negative thinking which could drown out the loving voice of God and His truth. We must ask ourselves where this negative thinking is birthed, because we do not have any difficulty hearing it! It certainly isn't in the mind of God, and yet at times we focus on these negatives thoughts and not on the word of the Father. We have an enemy who is determined to sabotage and damage our hearing, and we are encouraged to do something about it: 'We demolish arguments and every pretension that sets itself up against the knowledge of God, and we take captive every thought to make it obedient to Christ' (2 Cor. 10:5).

So how do we hear the right voice, God's voice? After all, prayer is God's idea; it is His gift to us. He longs to communicate with us and draw us to Himself, to impart His wisdom so we can live out our lives from a place of deep relationship with the God who lavishes His love on us (1 John 3:1). There may be times though when we might question if we really can hear the voice of God, but Jesus made it clear that He is close enough for us to listen: 'Jesus replied, "Anyone who loves me will obey my teaching. My Father will love them, and we will come to them and make our home with them"' (John 14:23, NIV 2011).

God has chosen to make His home within us, and we have been filled with His Holy Spirit who knows the mind of God! What an amazing revelation; the Spirit knows the mind of God and we have the Spirit: 'The Spirit searches all things, even the deep things of God. For who among men knows the thoughts of a man except the man's spirit within him? In the same way no-one knows the thoughts of God except the Spirit of God. We have not received the spirit of the world but the Spirit who is from God, that we may understand what God has freely given us' (1 Cor. 2:10–12).

We need to tune into the voice of God through the Spirit, who wants to whisper into our very being.

Pause to reflect

Do you spend time listening to God for yourself, and for others?

As we begin to look at the keys to hearing His voice, pray that God will really speak to you, and you will hear what He has to say.

Keys to hearing God's voice

1. Be still

'Be still, and know that I am God' (Psa. 46:10).
'Wait for the LORD; be strong and take heart and wait for the LORD' (Psa. 27:14).
Elijah was called out onto the mountain to experience the presence of the Lord, and God revealed something to him that gives us our first key.

> The LORD said, 'Go out and stand on the mountain in the presence of the LORD, for the LORD is about to pass by.' Then a great and powerful wind tore the mountains apart and shattered the rocks before the LORD, but the LORD was not in the wind. After the wind there was an earthquake, but the LORD was not in the earthquake. After the earthquake came a fire, but the LORD was not in the fire. And after the fire came a gentle whisper. When Elijah heard it, he pulled his cloak over his face and went out and stood at the mouth of the cave.
>
> 1 Kings 19:11–13

We need to be intentional about listening. If Elijah had not waited for the whisper, he might have missed God's encouragement and next purpose for him. We are called to 'be still' to 'wait for the LORD'. Sometimes it is so difficult to find the space in our busy schedules for time to be still long enough to experience that whisper. But getting alone with God and reading His Word nurtures our lives, restores our peace, feeds our souls, and gives us direction. We need to stay and not rush away. Sheila Walsh describes what it means for her to wait in the presence of the Lord:

My times of silence before God are very important to me now. I put everything else down, every word away, and I am with the Lord. When I am quiet, life falls into perspective for me. I have a very active mind and I'm a worrier, but in those moments when I choose to put that away, I rest beside the Shepherd in still places.[2]

I have found that choosing a special place to be still is conducive to hearing God speak to me. These places have changed over the years as our children have gone from babies to adults, and we have moved from home to home. My conservatory is a place where I can settle and experience peace, where I can see into the garden and feel the warmth of the sun. It is slightly detached from the rest of the house, and I know that I am unlikely to be disturbed. But when the children were small, a lunchtime *Sesame Street* programme gave me the time I needed, though I often found myself falling asleep. However, that may have even been a gift from the Father! I know a faithful woman who has a special chair she sits in early in the morning and waits on God before she begins her day. Some people find walking out in the country or by the sea gives them the ability to commune with God. I would encourage you to find that special place and settle into a quiet time, expecting to experience the Spirit whisper the Father's heart into your spirit.

Pause to reflect

How important is it for me to hear God's whisper to my heart? Where is my special place for listening to God? How can I be still and wait?

2. Use the eyes of your heart

I keep asking that the God of our Lord Jesus Christ, the glorious Father, may give you the Spirit of wisdom and revelation, so that you may know him better. I pray also that the eyes of your heart may be enlightened in order that you may know the hope to which he has called you, the riches of his glorious inheritance in the saints.

Eph. 1:17–18

When my children were small, they would spend hours building dens and playing out creative stories using their imaginations. As a primary school teacher, I really enjoyed encouraging the children to use their imaginations in creative writing and drama activities. What happens to us in our adult lives; do we forget to use our imaginations, or do the years of formal education and work prevent us from using them? I believe our creativity is a gift from God, something that as image-bearers we have inherited from Him. It is something that can enhance our prayer life and ability to hear God's voice. Mark Virkler in his book *Dialogue With God*[3] encourages us to 'see' what God is saying. Based on Habakkuk 2:1–2, he encourages us to use vision in our communication with God: 'I will stand at my watch and station myself on the ramparts; *I will look to see what he will say to me*, and what answer I am to give to this complaint' (Hab. 2:1, my italics). As someone who always found it difficult to hear God speak to him, Virkler spent time researching ways to help him communicate so he could enjoy the presence of God more intimately. He says: 'As I am before the Lord, I ask Him if there is anything He wants to show me and I deliberately present the eyes of my heart to Him, expecting Him to fill them with vision and revelation.'

Here it is again, the act of being deliberate. Quite often, when I am waiting before God, people, images and even scenes come into my imagination. I have learned not to ignore them, but to check them out and talk to God about them. A quickening in my spirit often confirms a need to respond. We only have to look at Jesus to know He did the same: 'Jesus gave them this answer: "I tell you the truth, the Son can do nothing by himself; he can do only what he sees his Father doing, because whatever the Father does the Son also does"' (John 5:19).

Jesus spoke in picture language. It engaged His audience and helped them to visualise the truth as well as hear it. Some of us find it more difficult than others to allow pictures to form in our minds. As someone who has a strong imagination, I was shocked when someone told me when they read a book they read the words but didn't imagine the characters! As I read the Gospels, I see Jesus walking among the crowd, I see His face as He speaks to people; I even try to hear how His voice sounds as He speaks. For me, it brings His ministry to life and I translate that into my communication with Him. Developing this gift of being able to use the 'eyes of our heart' requires time. Meditate on the words of Jesus and hear Him speaking them to you, using your name. He's that close.

Pause to reflect

Ask God to open the eyes of your heart. Imagine Jesus coming in and sitting next to you and enjoy the experience.

3. Write down what you hear and see

'My sheep listen to my voice; I know them, and they follow me' (John 10:27); 'Your own ears will hear him. Right behind you a voice will say, "This is the way you should go," whether to the right or to the left' (Isa. 30:21, NLT). As we tune in to hear God, we will get to know His voice. We have already said that we can easily hear negative voices; God's voice will always be encouraging and never condemning, even when He needs to teach us something to help us grow. We are each unique, and we need to understand how He will speak to us. Personally, I hear words and phrases during prayer times as well as during conversations and sermons. Scriptures stand out on the page as if I have never really seen them before; and sometimes pictures and people fire my imagination. I have heard it said that 'prayer is being caught in the flow of God'; what a wonderful thought. As His Spirit flows through us, we will catch something of the heart of the Father. Our conversation with Him is, after all, because we are in relationship with Him; a relationship built on love, and we want to hear what our Lover has to say.

One of the jokes in our family is that I don't have a great memory, so that even though my husband remembers every little detail of a conversation, I don't. I tend to have to write everything down in order to remind myself of tasks to accomplish, meetings with people, things I have promised to do and so on. It is the same with devotional times, for two reasons. If a stray thought comes in reminding me of something I need to do, I can write it down somewhere for later; more importantly, if God speaks, I want to remember what He has said, so I come to my time with Him with paper and pen, especially when I am asking for guidance. God advised Habakkuk and John to write down what they had seen and heard. 'Then the LORD replied: "Write down the revelation and make it plain on tablets so that a herald may run with it"' (Hab. 2:2); 'Write, therefore, what you have seen, what is now ...' (Rev. 1:19).

Writing down or journalling what we see and hear not only enables us to keep track of what God says, it helps us to process it and see how it builds into our lives. At times when I believe I have heard God speak, I can tend to think, 'This can't possibly be meant for me.' Fear and doubt can rob us of the wonderful things God has in store for us. Sharing these things with prayer partners or people with experience can help. There is a tendency for some of us to filter God's words through our sense of inadequacy, inexperience, or memories of past failures; other people can help us to bring these things into perspective.

I woke one morning, and during a time of prayer felt quite clearly that God was encouraging me to stage a women's conference. I had the title, theme, venue, plan and speaker in my mind and heart as a visual experience. I wrote the whole plan down with words and pictures and was feeling very excited about it. Then I filtered it through my inexperience and began to doubt I had heard correctly. I decided to pray with a very experienced Christian woman who caught the vision immediately, and a new area of our women's ministry was born. Potentially I could have been robbed of seeing the blessing of God's plan in not only my life, but also in the lives of other women. I could have listened to the wrong voice. Writing the plan down somehow brought life and coherence to the thoughts; it made sense to me as I read it.

Jesus knew we would face this kind of challenge. Nowhere is it more prevalent than when we are asking for God to speak to us, when we are looking for revelation of who He is and what He wants to say:

Jesus said to them, 'If God were your Father, you would love me, for I have come here from God. I have not come on my own; God sent me. Why is my language not clear to you? Because you are unable to hear what I say. You belong to your father, the devil, and you want to carry out your father's desires. He was a murderer from the beginning, not holding to the truth, for there is no truth in him. When he lies, he speaks his native language, for he is a liar and the father of lies. Yet because I tell the truth, you do not believe me!'

John 8:42–45, NIV 2011

Pause to reflect

Expect to hear God's voice. Learn to tune in to the Father's voice. Write down thoughts, phrases, scriptures that 'speak' to you. Draw pictures or diagrams that represent what you've heard.

God's voice is the voice of truth; it draws us into a place of security and brings us life. He takes us to a place of love, joy and peace, yet He encourages us to step out in faith and into our future. Listening to God in the stillness, using our minds and the eyes of our hearts will enrich our experience of knowing Him and take us to a deeper level of understanding.

NOTES

1. Patsy Clairmont, *Adventurous Prayer* (Women of Faith Study Guide) (Nashville, TN: Thomas Nelson Publishers, 2003).
2. Quoted in Patsy Clairmong, *Adventurous Prayer* (Women of Faith Study Guide) (Nashville, TN: Thomas Nelson Publishers, 2003).
3. Mark Virkler, *Dialogue with God* (South Plainfield, NJ: Bridge Publishing, 1994).

PART 3:

Practical Working
with Others

UNDERSTANDING YOURSELF AND OTHERS

Lynn Penson

Do you find all the groups you are part of work together in perfect harmony? No arguments, misunderstandings, quiet resentments? If that is the case, this chapter is not for you. However, my guess is that, like me, you find those little irritations and difficulties simmering quietly much of the time, and on occasions rising above the surface causing tension and hurt – even when the group you are with share a common Christian faith.

Imagine the scene

You are responsible for a women's group in your church. Tonight it is being held in Sally's home and is a 'Puddings and Quiz' social night organised by Helen, one of your committee members.

You arrive in good time to find that Sally is still putting the children to bed, with the sink and draining board full of dishes and the children's toys and clothes scattered everywhere. Helen arrives, laden with puddings and a pile of quiz-type papers that need posting around the living room. She complains loudly that there is nowhere to put anything. Sally sweetly suggests that anywhere will do, before racing back upstairs with a storybook.

The women start arriving. You have a good idea who will arrive early, who will be late and who will arrive just at the right time, and you are proved right. You are also right about Jenny, who arrives an hour late even though she had offered to bring nibbles for the beginning of the evening, and about Sue, who phoned up just half an hour before the evening began to ask if it was all right to come even though she hadn't signed up by yesterday's deadline.

The evening progresses with Anna talking loudly and Sarah saying nothing. Sue comments that the cream on the pavlova has gone off, whilst Helen says it is perfect, though you notice she has left all but a mouthful. Judy spends the entire evening in the kitchen clearing up first Sally's dishes, then the evening's washing up, and then slips away without anyone knowing. Anna stays so late chatting that Sally goes to bed and leaves you to work out how to entice her to leave.

You think back over the evening as you climb in to bed. It was a lovely social event, but you can't help thinking, 'Why can't people be more like me?'!

Myers-Briggs

Sometimes differences in other people can be easily tolerated, accepted and welcomed, but undoubtedly at other times they can create friction. If you are leading any group, you will find this a cause of tension at times.

There are a number of aids to helping us understand the differences between ourselves and others. One that I am trained in and have found invaluable over many years is the Myers-Briggs Type Indicator™. I like this because not only does it help me appreciate who I am, but it also gives me the tools to appreciate and value those different from me. I might still struggle and get frustrated, and it has not resulted in my perfect acceptance of others, but it has certainly aided me greatly in my relationships.

The Myers-Briggs Type Indicator™ looks at four areas of our personality, putting them together to allocate each person as one of sixteen 'types'. This is not to say that you then are labelled or boxed in; quite the reverse. If understood and used properly it should not limit you, but is a means of helping you grow and expand your horizons. Also, it is important to remember that there are great differences even within each of the sixteen types. And the many other influences and experiences of life will bring numerous different shades to each category. In addition, it requires us to understand that this is not about what we can and cannot do, but is about preference; what, when left freely to our natural devices, we would prefer to do in most situations and so generally what we do best.

As we explore this, we proceed with some caution, remembering that this must be understood simply as one of many tools to help us to gain a better understanding of ourselves and other people, and how to relate to, and work with, others better.

Pause to reflect

Before you begin to look at the piece below, pray that God would speak to you and give you discernment in regards to yourself, and to others.

Active Annie or Reflective Rita?

One area the MBTI looks at is what gives us energy and stimulates us; whether, as in the case of extraverts, it is the outer world, or for introverts, the inner world.

My personal preference is for extraversion. I am drawn outwards to what is going on around me, and so doing things and being with other people give me energy. It also means that the things I think and feel tend to be 'out there' for all to see and hear. I tend to say what I am thinking, sometimes wishing that I had thought a little more about it first. I like being with people and feel stifled with too much of my own company. I am usually more than happy to be interrupted by the phone or the pinging of my inbox. People who are like me in this respect will often be good in group discussion and activity, though some of us will be prone to dominate discussions if we carry on without thought of others. We may be better at talking than listening; I have had to train myself to focus without letting my attention wander to conversations happening elsewhere.

My 'opposite', with a preference for introversion, is not so at ease with outer demands and intrusions and needs time alone to re-energise. Their thoughts and feelings tend to be kept inside much more, and they may take their time to voice their opinions, or not even express them at all, so may seem more difficult to really get to know. They may often be rather reserved in group discussions. Being with other people constantly will drain the introvert. They are often good at listening, or at least appear so, but not so easy with chit-chat, finding social occasions more demanding – even stressful at times.

There is a great danger when these two apparent opposites misunderstand and so misjudge others. An introvert may feel resentful of the extravert, who always seems to have something to say but rarely asks for their opinion. They may also feel frustrated at constant interruptions to their flow of thought. Conversely, the extravert may feel the introvert is being antisocial by not always joining in activities or conversations and so withdraw their friendship. When each understands the other's approach to life, those tensions can be replaced by valuing and appreciating what different types bring to the group.

Next time you get together in a group, look out for those who are quiet, and ensure that the more talkative ones give them opportunity to voice their opinions. Equally, give space for the extraverts to share their thoughts, even before fully formed, and encourage them to recognise and value the differences in their personalities.

Down-to-earth Dora or Intuitive Irene?

Another area of difference highlighted by the MBTI is how we take in information and how we perceive people and the world around us.

Some of us will be very sensing, relying on our senses such as sight, hearing and sense of touch. We live in the present and tend to be very practical. Sensing people will tend to be careful about facts and details, and like things to progress in a sequential way, so will start at the beginning and work a step at a time.

Others of us will tend to be more intuitive, more interested in future possibilities than facts, liking change and variety and becoming bored if needing to do the same task repeatedly. There is a tendency to jump in anywhere, whether it is a conversation, a book, a job to be done, or instructions to be followed. Imagination and creativity are valued and enjoyed by these people; for intuitive types it doesn't matter so much what *it is* now as much as what it *could become.*

When these two types get together it can seem as if they are talking different languages, one being from the world of the here and now, the other from the world of what is possible or yet to come.

In your groups, encourage people to see the strengths of both approaches, and how the down-to-earth types have a role in enabling the vision of the intuitive to happen in a realistic way. Encourage those future-orientated folk to recognise that their visions need to be based on the situation as it is here and now.

Thinking Thora or Feeling Freda?

The way we make decisions is a third area of difference; do we make decisions based on objective logic and analysis, as thinker-deciders, or on more subjective values, as feeler-deciders?

As a feeler-decider, I will tend to be driven by my feelings, and readily consider the feelings of others. I put myself in the shoes of other people and want them to feel comfortable and appreciated. This being the case, I dislike conflict, seeing it as interrupting harmony, and also find that making decisions that negatively impact people is extremely disturbing. I have learned to welcome criticism, but this has not been easy; feeler-deciders tend to take criticism very personally. They will tend to think, 'If you don't like my dress, my house, my way of doing things, then you cannot like *me.*' This can make us difficult to work and live with when difficult issues have to be addressed, and we can become overly emotional at times.

Thinker-deciders will usually be able to tackle difficult issues with people more readily because they are able to take the long view, and respond more easily to people's thoughts and ideas rather than their feelings. They find criticism easier to take, providing it is fair and correct. Their natural ability to find flaws can be disconcerting for people who may feel hurt by their comments and suggestions.

They will tend to be more concerned with truth, where their opposite is more concerned with tact.

In your groups, encourage your 'Feeling Fredas' to value the 'Thinking Thoras'; this is especially important in an all-female group, where the tendency is to be stronger feelers and to see the thinkers as not caring enough. Recognise that there are different ways of showing care. Those thinkers may need to recognise how easy it is to hurt someone if enough consideration is not taken in expressing what they see as being simply truthful comments.

Decided Deirdre or Flexible Flora?

How we live and plan our lives is the fourth and often most contentious area.

Some of us will like to have all of life under control, and that probably includes controlling other people's lives too. We like things to be well organised, live by the rule of 'a place for everything and everything in its place' and tend to deal with deadlines well in advance. We like to work through our 'to-do' list, and it may even give us great satisfaction to cross off items as we complete them. We like decisions to be made and settled. We may seem inflexible and demanding to our more flexible friends and colleagues who don't want to rush into decisions. For them, being tied down by lists, agendas and schedules feels restricting and they are more comfortable going with the flow, experiencing life as it happens and being open to change and to new things. They are more at ease with uncertainties and tend to be adaptable.

If we don't understand this very fundamental difference, we will not understand why some people need to know details well in advance while others find it difficult to plan ahead of the deadline.

In your groups, encourage people to value these different lifestyles, recognising that both orderliness and flexibility are necessary when working with others.

Pause to reflect

What has God shown you as you have read through the paragraphs above? Think of ways in which you could encourage others in your group to recognise and value differences.

Using the knowledge

If we do not recognise these intrinsic differences in our natures, we will find ourselves getting frustrated with others and being the source of irritation to other people. At times we might find ourselves criticising others for not being more like us, or berating ourselves for not being more like others. Many groups struggle in their relationships due to personality issues, and people feeling judged or misunderstood.

If we can learn to understand both ourselves and others better, we can value those differences between us rather than allow them to become a cause of annoyance. We can help ourselves by balancing those areas where we are not so strong with the help of those people who have different strengths to us.

A word of caution. These descriptions are not given in order to label ourselves or others. They are about *tendencies*, and *preference*. We will not be 100 per cent one or the other, and we are not restricted to always acting in the ways suggested above.

We are encouraged by New Testament writers to recognise and value our different gifts and abilities, to live together in peace and to remember that we all have a part to play in the Body of Christ. One excellent piece of advice as we consider our exploration of differences in others comes from Paul in his letter to the Philippians: 'Finally, brothers and sisters, whatever is true, whatever is noble, whatever is right, whatever is pure, whatever is lovely, whatever is admirable – if anything is excellent or praiseworthy – think about such things' (Phil. 4:8, NIV 2011).

CROSSING CULTURES

Gail Dixon

In the beginning ...

Wouldn't it be great if we all spoke the same language? Have you ever felt like that, when you couldn't make yourself understood? That is how it was when humankind was young, at a place called Babel. Language and culture has its roots in what happened there (see Gen. 11:1–9).

People gathered together to build a tower to reach the heavens. Their goal was to make a name for themselves. They turned the whole purpose of God on its head. He had never meant us to try by our own efforts to somehow reach heaven and make a name for ourselves. His plan was for us to partner with Him, showing His name to be holy, and to bring heaven down to earth.

The Lord confused the languages at that time, and we still reap the effects today. However, something amazing happened on the day of Pentecost recorded in Acts chapter 2, reversing what happened at Babel for those who will choose to walk in the power of the Holy Spirit.

Instead of people aspiring to make a name for themselves, God found a group of people doing what Jesus had taught them to do, hallowing (making holy, venerating, lifting high) His name. They were all together, united and devoting themselves to prayer. The Holy Spirit came; and they found themselves speaking in languages they had never learned. Instead of confusion, there was an incredible order, because each person listening heard about the mighty works of God in their own native tongue.

Through the Holy Spirit, barriers of language and culture were being broken. Though all these people were Jews, or proselytes to Judaism, they came from every corner of the then known world. They would have had many different customs and cultures. Heaven was coming down to earth, and God's purpose was being restored. The result was that 3,000 people from all these different backgrounds found salvation on the same day. And that was only the beginning.

Resistance

OK, it should be easy, then! We should be able to cross these barriers of language and culture without too much difficulty. But we all know that is not the reality. So why is there such resistance in us? Even in the Early Church, with the first powerful move of the Holy Spirit, they struggled. The Lord had told them: 'you will receive power when the Holy Spirit comes on you; and you will be my witnesses in Jerusalem, and in all Judea and Samaria, and to the ends of the earth' (Acts 1:8).

So, when the Holy Spirit came, what did they do? They witnessed in Jerusalem. Yes, they broke through some cultural barriers where they were, but they stayed in Jerusalem. It was not until they were forced out by persecution that the Church took the gospel to Judea and Samaria.

What keeps us in our own circles, even when we love the Lord and are filled with His Spirit? If we can identify these things and see them as enemies of the gospel, and therefore *our* enemies, we can begin to overcome them.

The apostle Paul proclaimed: 'I am not ashamed of the gospel, because it is the power of God for the salvation of everyone who believes: first for the Jew, then for the Gentile' (Rom. 1:16).

Pause to reflect

What keeps you in your own circle of friends and family?

Do you ever 'break out'? How might you share your faith with those of different cultural backgrounds?

Unbelief

Unbelief is the root of every sin (see John 16:9; Rom. 14:23). Paul knew that the whole power of God was behind him every time he shared the gospel, whether it was to a Jew or a Gentile (someone from any other nation or culture). Do we know this power? Do we see someone behind a veil, or with a turban on their head, and think, even subconsciously, that they would never become a Christian? We listen to the little voice in our minds which says, 'They wouldn't want to talk to me' or 'I don't understand anything about their beliefs, or their culture. How can I talk to them?' We allow unbelief to be our tutor. We feel inadequate, and tell ourselves that someone else who is more qualified can witness to them. I wonder how many people have died without hearing the gospel because we haven't grasped the power that the gospel has to break down every barrier. Let's kick out unbelief and choose to take God at His word.

Fear

Fear is another of our enemies. In today's world many equate Islam with terrorism. Even the Church is tainted with this fear of Muslims. A fifth of the world's population is now Muslim. They are people with the same longings and the same struggles as us. Many have suffered prejudice and are now wary of non-Muslims. Satan is erecting fear barriers in every way that he can.

We are naturally afraid of the unknown. We hate being vulnerable. Even if we dare to approach someone of another culture and belief, we would like to go armed with all the answers. However, vulnerability in any relationship is an asset. No one likes a 'know-it-all'. People don't like to be preached at. We need to free ourselves to realise that we don't have to have all the answers.

We are all, no matter what culture or faith we come from, hungry for love. Love is our weapon – 'perfect love drives out fear' (1 John 4:18). Yet it is a most uncomfortable weapon. It will keep us in the place of honesty and vulnerability. Jesus came and made friends, not converts.

Selfishness

Selfishness is perhaps the other major barrier to us breaking out of our comfort zone and befriending people from other cultures. It is easier to stay with what and who we know. It takes effort to try to communicate with someone who does not speak our language very well – and takes even more effort to learn their language. Then there are all the misunderstandings that come as soon as we try to cross into someone else's culture. We invite them for a meal at 7pm and they turn up with a big smile and a few extra members of the family at nearly 8pm! We are trying our best to be polite, and they take deep offence because we haven't used the correct gesture or word. Then, when we are invited to their house, our stomach churns at the dish they set before us.

It is only too real, as I can testify from years of working cross-culturally. Even on the mission field it is easy to retreat into a ghetto of our home culture rather than push out every day into the unknown.

And yet, there is Someone who suffered a greater culture shock than any of us could ever imagine:

> Tender strength, the uncreated One
> contains Himself in frail flesh and blood,
> life pulse of Life, breath of all breathing things,
> submits to form to manifest His Love.
>
> The WORD, a cry until He learns to speak;
> the LIGHT, a flame that few will recognise;
> the WAY is carried in His mother's arms;
> TRUTH in a single child, GRACE realised.
>
> The POWER, led humbled to a cruel death;
> the LOVER, left forsaken in the grave.
> The INNOCENT, defiled becoming Sin,
> yet in His greatest weakness, strong to save.

Tender strength, the Firstborn from the dead
breaks through the gates of hell in flesh and blood.
And death bows down, graves open, chains fall off
releasing us to be children of God!

What a model we have! The Creator of all things, God of heaven and earth, compelled by love. He held nothing back. He identified completely with human culture, being born into a simple family and growing up in a town that was despised, Nazareth (John 1:46). Even His ancestry was 'suspect'. He did not have pure Jewish blood. Ruth, a Moabitess, and Rahab, a Canaanite prostitute, were in His lineage. He came to an occupied nation, and lived an obscure life for thirty years. Yet, much more than that, in the three years that followed, He demonstrated the culture of heaven and paid the price for everything negative in our cultures and in our natures.

There is a cost to crossing a culture. But One has gone before us who has paid with His life to cross into *our* culture. Can we dare hold back because we are inconvenienced to cross into someone else's?

Pause to reflect

Meditate for a while on the huge cultural leap Jesus made when He came to earth from heaven. See how much He loves you. Let His love expose any selfishness, fear and unbelief in you. Let Him take down the barriers that stop you ministering to others.

The culture of the cross

For he himself is our peace, who has made the two one and has destroyed the barrier, the dividing wall of hostility, by abolishing in his flesh the law with its commandments and regulations. His purpose was to create in himself one new man out of the two, thus making peace.

Eph. 2:14–15

Jesus died to break down the dividing wall of hostility between different cultures. He died to bring us into one body, His Body. There is a new culture that He embraced to unite us, and that is the culture of the cross. Jesus delights in our diversity; after all, He created each of us to be unique – our fingerprints, our DNA, our voices, our faces and, more importantly, our souls (our minds, our wills, our emotions) and our spirits. Each of us was lovingly fashioned in our mother's womb by the Divine hand. Each of us has a distinctive work and calling from our Creator.

As with individuals, so with nations. Each nation has an inheritance and a destiny. We see it in Scripture. We are told Cush (Ethiopia) will submit to God (Psa. 68:31). The prophet Isaiah speaks of Egypt, Assyria (Iran, Syria and Eastern Turkey) with Israel being a blessing on the earth (19:24), Sheba (Yemen) bringing gold and proclaiming God's praises (60:6), the islands looking to Him (60:9).

The Lord has given each individual, and each nation, strengths that are meant to blend beautifully together into one glorious bride. He invites us to submit our own cultures to the culture of the cross. We do not lose who we are as we do this; in fact, the cross releases who we are really created to be, whether as an individual or as a nation. All this works towards one great, final destiny. The book of Revelation tries to picture it in many ways for us. Here is one: 'After this I looked and there before me was a great multitude that no-one could count, from every nation, tribe, people and language, standing before the throne and in front of the Lamb' (Rev. 7:9).

As we focus on the Lamb, we will want to cross cultures and languages so that He will have the reward of His sufferings and be satisfied. As we see Him, we will embrace the culture of the cross.

Pause to reflect

You may like to spend some time focusing on Jesus, thanking Him for the uniqueness and the individuality of people and nations. Thank Him for who you are and the purpose He has for your life. Ask Him to show you how to embrace the culture of the cross in your walk with Him today.

Practicalities

How do we begin to get to know someone who is so completely different to us?

1. Focus on what we have in common

There will be more areas than you think. It is best whenever possible to go woman-to-woman, and leave the men to other men. These women have the same basic concerns that we all do: family, finances, children's education and well-being etc. Smiling and being friendly is always a good first step. As you pray for them the Lord will show 'natural' ways to continue the relationship. It could be as simple as inviting her in for a cup of tea, or seeing if she would like to come shopping with you. If she is in a minority culture in your area, the chances are she will be lonely and longing for company and kindness.

2. Be vulnerable

Every relationship is a two-way thing. We need to be willing to learn at least as much as we are 'teaching'. As Christians, we usually want to present ourselves as having everything sorted out in our lives. That can be very intimidating for someone who is feeling vulnerable. Often the response will be that she puts up barriers so as not to expose herself. Be honest, be real. That does not of course mean burdening her with all your problems. However, if a genuine friendship is to develop, there will need to be mutual vulnerability which gives a basis for growing trust. When I worked in North Africa, a friend caught me crying one day. I was very embarrassed at first, and felt that I had let down the cause of the gospel. However, after that time my relationship with my friend deepened, and she later confided that she was so relieved to realise that I cried too.

3. Practise acts of kindness

Kindness is one of the fruit of the Spirit. It speaks directly to the heart, crossing every language barrier. Ask the Holy Spirit how His kindness can flow through you to your new friend. Listen to what she says, really see her situation, and it will not be long before you will find opportunities.

4. Show respect for who she is, where she comes from and what she believes

One simple way to do this is to learn a few words of your friend's language, even if it is only the greetings. Ask her about her country and her beliefs. Eat what she cooks. As you learn about her it is very likely that she will want to learn about you. Don't worry that you may not know anything of her religion. Let her teach you. Be careful not to speak against something that she believes. You don't need to agree with her, but it is important that she knows that you are listening and respecting her.

When you get an opportunity to speak of your faith, try to keep things personal. You don't need to launch into the 'Four Spiritual Laws of Salvation', but just tell her how you met Jesus and what He means to you. Testimony is inoffensive and powerful. Gauge how much to say by how interested she is. Don't force a conversation. Be prepared to take time and wait for the opportunities.

Check your own heart constantly for any prejudice. It is amazing how deep-rooted prejudice is in our thinking. I was shocked to find it in myself, even though I was a missionary; I found myself believing that somehow I was superior to the village girls I was among. It was not a conscious emotion at first. The Holy Spirit had to uncover it in me layer by layer. I was horrified at the discovery and had to repent deeply.

5. Expect the power of God to be manifested

You are not alone as you befriend this lady. The whole force of heaven is cheering you on. Jesus told the disciples that when they were welcomed into anyone's home they could leave their peace in that place (Matt. 10:13). It may not be appropriate at first for you to pray openly, but you can silently bless the home and leave your peace. As the friendship grows, she will confide her struggles to you. Offer to pray for her. Have faith that the Lord will demonstrate His love to her as you pray. Miracles of healing, for example, are meant as a testimony to unbelievers: 'And these signs will accompany those who believe: ... they will place their hands on sick people, and they will get well' (Mark 16:17–18).

I have travelled quite extensively and worked in various cultures, and it is very rare that anyone refuses prayer, as long as we present ourselves with sensitivity and love. People want to be blessed. We have the power to bless them.

Pause to reflect

Think of someone you know from another culture, no matter how vaguely, and ask the Lord how you can use the points above to begin to form a meaningful relationship with her. Expect God to anoint you and release His power as you step out in faith.

Groups

I have been talking here mainly of an individual crossing a culture for the sake of the gospel. However, there is multiplied power in a church or a group of people working together to cross cultures. Broadly speaking, we can divide cultures into Eastern and Western. Eastern is largely group- and family-orientated whereas Western is individualistic. By far the majority of people belong to an Eastern culture. The importance of community and family to make Eastern people feel welcomed cannot be underestimated.

Some examples of events churches or groups have set up to welcome different cultures into their community are:

- Language learning (whether official courses or just conversational help)
- International evenings, celebrating the food, music and cultures of different groups
- Practical help teams; everything from how to register at the doctors' to finding enough baby clothes for new refugees

In the Central African Republic, one team went into the rainforest and set up schools, a pharmacy, a farming project and a church for the Pygmies. In previous generations, the Central Africans had enslaved the Pygmy population. Chinese believers are serving Tibetans, whose land and culture has been devastated by their government. Jews are blessing Palestinians and vice versa.

Barriers are coming down as people embrace the culture of the cross.

'You are all sons of God through faith in Christ Jesus, for all of you who were baptised into Christ have clothed yourselves with Christ. There is neither Jew nor Greek, slave nor free, male nor female, for you are all one in Christ Jesus' (Gal. 3:26–28). Paul triumphantly declares we are all sons, because we have been baptised into Christ, the Son. Women have the full right of sons. African and Chinese, American and Arab are one in Christ. The poorest and the most powerful are one in Christ.

We live in a broken world, but we hold the answer to its suffering within us. We can start, step by step, day by day, choosing to embrace the culture of the cross. As we do that, we hallow the name of the Father, and see His kingdom coming and His will being done on earth as it is in heaven.

Designed for Living

Jeannette Barwick

One of the most exciting and empowering concepts we can pursue in the Christian life is the biblical fact that, as persons, we are made to function according to a divine design. Soon after joining CWR in the 1980s, I was exposed to their biblical teaching on how God made us and what makes us tick. My own life has been greatly impacted by understanding the implications of what it means to be made in God's image. I have been released from old patterns of living as I have come to understand more clearly how God has made me, and this has enabled me to find my identity in who I am in Christ in an ever-deepening way. Because of this, I want to share those implications with you.

The image of God

What does it really mean to be made in the image of God? And how does understanding this fact empower us in our spiritual lives? I want to try to pull the whole thing into clear focus for you. God has made us with five distinct areas of functioning. We are:

- physical beings
- longing beings
- thinking beings

- choosing beings
- feeling beings.

These different capacities are not designed to work in isolation from one another, but in wonderful integration. The better we understand each of these areas of functioning and the way in which they fit together, the better we will understand what is involved in growing more and more into the divine likeness.

It is important to understand right from the start that God's overall purpose for our lives is that we should function in the way Christ did when He was on this planet. He was the greatest model of how life should be lived that the world has ever seen. The fact that God wants us to be like Him is clearly portrayed in that wonderful verse in Romans 8:29, which the Living Bible paraphrases in this way: 'For from the very beginning God decided that those who came to him ... should become like his Son'. God is so thrilled with Jesus that He wants to make everyone like Him; not in appearance, of course, but in the way we live and function.

One of the great joys of my life has been to take these concepts and present them to hundreds of women in the Designer Living (Designed for Living) seminar. Nothing is more satisfying to me, as a teacher of biblical truth, than to spend time helping women discover their true identity in Christ. And I have found that nothing empowers a woman more than understanding what it truly means to be made in the image of God and to live in this transforming experience – a way of living that is truly Christ-empowered.

Deep longings and chosen goals

In order to understand the way God designed us to function, we need to reflect on that wonderful statement in Genesis 1:26 and 27 which reads, 'Then God said, "Let us make man in our image, in our likeness ... " ... male and female he created them.' The first thing that God provided for humankind was a body, and into that body He put the image of Himself. Humanity was able to think like God, feel like God, and choose like God. Central to all this was the fact that God placed within their spirits a longing for Himself, ensuring that apart from a relationship with Him their spirits would never be fully satisfied.

We are made in such a way that unless God is resident at the core of our being then our thinking, choosing and feeling capacities will not function in the way our Divine Designer intended. Our human personalities were set up to think and to choose in harmony with God's will, the result of which would be that we would not struggle with debilitating feelings. The whole reason why we have difficulties in the way we function is because we do not allow God to take over control of our inner being, which then affects our thinking and our choices so that we try to meet the inner emptiness with something other than God. If we could put a stethoscope on the core of our beings, we would discover, I believe, three great longings – a longing to be loved, a longing to be valued, and a longing for our lives to have meaning. We sometimes refer to these longings as the desire for security, self-worth and significance respectively.

What is so empowering about all this? Let Sally's testimony after she had attended a CWR seminar help put things in perspective. She learned the concept that unless God is meeting the deep needs of our spirits, we choose alternative goals for those needs to be met which, when they become blocked, or are uncertain or unreachable, produce in us emotions of anger and resentment, fear and anxiety, or guilt and shame:

> … Selwyn Hughes talked about the MCs (Miserable Christians) and I immediately related. Then he went on to ask 'What are your core beliefs? That is, what do you say to yourself, "for me to live is …"?' And I've had to admit, harmless though it may sound, that one major drive has been to live for my white conscience. This has led to patterns of crazy, defensive living, taking few if any risks, rarely voicing opinions and generally skirting areas that might mean taking responsibility for making mistakes – which makes for negative uncreative living. Ask my husband and children!
>
> I can write humorously but the reality is far from funny. It becomes an insane world where mentally you

back track over events and can never forgive yourself. You try to control and manipulate people and events to be 'right'. You completely miss the bigger picture in this obsessive preoccupation to perform perfectly and who in the end is on the throne of the heart – God or self?

I heard that emotions like guilt or shame represent a warning that we have set ourselves a goal that is unreachable. We are looking for our significance, our self-worth and our security in that goal rather than in God. And that, as we repent of this wrong thinking and make it our goal to please Him (2 Cor 5:9) – which is a goal that can never be blocked – God not only changes our wrong thinking but sets us free from this wrong idol.

And God does set us free. It's a slow journey but I am gradually discovering quiet times that focus on God (rather than being sessions in self-condemnation), learning how to worship (which for me now includes singing), and realising how loaded the Bible is with God's promises to renew our minds. Bit by bit, he is healing my negative patterns of thinking.[1]

Pause to reflect

'A longing to be loved, a longing to be valued, and a longing for our lives to have meaning.' How does this resonate with you? Take an honest look and consider how these needs are being met in your own life. Pray that as you come to a deeper understanding of this for yourself, so you will be able to minister to the deep needs of others, by the power of the Spirit of God.

The bottom line is that if we do not allow God to meet our basic needs for security, self-worth and significance, then we will pursue other routes in our attempt to meet those needs in our own way – we will think and choose other sources of satisfaction – and so upset our ability to function in the way God designed us.

For further illustration, take the case of a woman who came to me at a Designer Living seminar in London, saying, 'I had always thought – well this is me, I can't change. I'll never be any different. I've been married for thirty years, and been a deacon in my church for fifteen. But now I can see that if I live in harmony with God's design, my way of living can be so different. It's a real revelation, and for the first time I've got a sense of hope. I feel like a new person!'

This woman's approach to her situation had enabled her just to survive – and many Christians seem content with this level of living. But with her new understanding came the confident hope that in and through Christ she could really *thrive*. And that is the intention of God.

Self-image

Clearly our creative God made us for creative growth, and it is His intention that we grow spiritually every day of our lives. It is wonderful to see women being released from old patterns of living as they have understood, often for the first time, how marvellously God has made them, and how the Bible shows us that the same characteristics we see in Christ can be seen in our lives also.

Returning to Genesis, let us consider the fact that God made man and woman in His own image. In chapter 3 we see that Adam and Eve made a choice in the Garden of Eden that was not in harmony with their original design. Prior to the first human pair making the wrong choice, if you were to draw lines from them up into infinity, you would have a fairly clear picture of God's nature and the way He functions. In their sinless state, they were true image-bearers who reflected God perfectly. Although we cannot expect to reflect God's image in the way Adam and Eve did before the Fall, it is certainly possible through Christ's residency and Lordship in our hearts to come closer.

The image of God, which could be seen in the lives of Adam and Eve before they sinned, meant that seeing God clearly, they saw themselves clearly. They perceived themselves in the way God did, as loved, valued and highly esteemed. Thus their self-image was healthy and balanced. However, after they had sinned they began to see themselves in a different light, and covered themselves with leaves because of the inner disturbance that their sin had brought about in their personalities.

One of the reasons for a negative self-image is that we do not live up to the design that our Creator has built into us. When we live according to that design, then we experience an inner contentment that has a tremendous effect on the way we perceive ourselves.

One of the biggest problems I have come across in my interactions with women is that of low self-image. It is high on the list of the most troublesome issues with which women have to contend. Linked with this is another interesting thing I have noticed in trying to help them with their problems; it is the way our body image affects our self-image. I have met few women who are really satisfied and content with their physical bodies. In today's world great emphasis is being placed on physical appearance, and the more emphasis the media places on this, the more discontented women (and young girls, too) are about the way they appear.

Pause to reflect

How affected are you by the media's portrayal of women? Is there anything you should bring to God, before you begin to minister freedom to others?

Physical beings

We need to safeguard our bodies by taking care of them. This doesn't mean seeking to attain physical perfection (were such a thing possible), nor does it mean becoming obsessed with the body in any way. It simply means respecting ourselves as God's creation, and being responsible about the way we look after ourselves.

When our body goes wrong, it can greatly influence the way we feel about ourselves. Our physiology can affect our psychology. A virus can cause depression; sometimes when a woman has a baby she can experience depression; significant sleep loss can produce hallucinations, and even banging your thumb can alter your world-view for a few moments. It works the other way round, too. A disturbance or stress in the soul can cause problems in our bodies. Our doctors have come up with a good word to explain this – psychosomatic; *psyche* meaning soul and *soma* meaning body.

The fact that our bodies are affected in this way is an enemy of spiritual growth. Whilst acknowledging that some do have significant physical issues to contend with, we need to ensure that, as far as is possible, we function well physically. If you thought that you could thrive spiritually without considering the importance of the physical, then think again. God has given each of us a body that we must treat with respect. Our soul is housed in a body, and we have a responsibility to take good care of it.

We need to do three things in relation to our physical bodies – exercise, eat healthily and adopt the right attitudes. In terms of exercise, our bodies were made to move, and even if we're not very energetic types, regular walking is good exercise. Secondly, we need to examine our eating habits and eat enough to keep us fit but not enough to make us fat. Thirdly, our attitudes are as important as our arteries, for just as the physical affects our moods and attitudes, so our moods and attitudes can affect the physical. It's not just what you eat, but what's eating you!

Cosmetic surgery has become increasingly popular these days, and many women seek to redesign some aspect of their physical form. Dr Maxwell Maltz was a plastic surgeon who spent many years rebuilding the faces of burns victims and remodelling facial features. As time went by, however, he discovered that even though he changed people's external appearance for the better, it didn't necessarily help them to feel any better about themselves. He went on to train as a psychologist so that he could help people more effectively by helping them to change on the inside. You see, it's not what we see in the mirror that affects us, it's what we *think* we see in the mirror that impacts us most powerfully.

Pause to reflect

Do you exercise, eat healthy and have the right attitudes? Is anything 'eating you'? How might you minister Christ's concern to someone who is clearly adopting an unhealthy lifestyle, to their own detriment?

Thinking beings

The way we think is one of the most important and determinative aspects of our human functioning. What we think affects the way we feel, and what we feel affects the choices we make and the way we behave. Scripture entreats us to 'be transformed by the renewing of your mind' (Rom. 12:2). So often our thoughts are completely out of kilter with God's thoughts about us, and it is of vital importance that we examine our self-talk.

Jenny discovered

> The number of thoughts that go through our minds in a given day is astounding – we certainly would not be able to speak at the rate of our thoughts! Yet, are all our thoughts helpful? Do they reflect reality? Understanding the 'thought-catching module' helped me to distinguish between useful thoughts, and thoughts that can provoke emotions that, in turn, can cause me to act in certain ways. In a sense we need to learn how to [talk] to ourselves. 'Why am I thinking that? What is behind this emotion? This is what I think – but what does Jesus think about this? What does His Word tell me is true?' This way, catching our thoughts and really examining them can bring real life change ... most of our behaviours stem from a thought or belief [that] we have perhaps unwittingly internalised as true ... How and what we think determines the direction in which we will look to have our deep longings for security, self-worth and significance met.[2]

And if the way to our chosen goal is then blocked, we will experience debilitating emotions. A blocked goal is most often the cause of negative emotions rising up within us – especially anger and resentment.

Pause to reflect

How aware are you of what you say to yourself? If your self-talk is negative and irrational and not based on biblical truth, it will result in negative emotions. Spend time 'thought catching', identifying your self-talk, and challenge any wrong thoughts with what God's Word says.

Feeling beings

This brings us to consider another part of the personality – our feelings. Generally speaking, women are very much more aware than men that we are feeling beings. We are usually very aware of our feelings. I do not think it extreme to say that there are times when our emotions threaten to overwhelm us, and many of our responses in life are emotionally driven. Have you ever wished God had created you with an on/off switch? When your emotions go into overload, wouldn't it be great just to turn them off? Oh, the bliss of being able to flick a switch and have serenity return!

Did you realise that an emotion, more often than not, is a response to a dominant thought? Keep in mind that a helpful way of understanding how troublesome emotions arise is to view them as the result of a failure to reach a predetermined goal – a goal which we believe we have got to reach in order to feel good about ourselves.

If I believe that being successful in my teaching ministry will meet my longings for security, self-worth and significance, I will look to my work for God rather to God Himself to meet my needs. Our thoughts powerfully influence the way we live our lives and the kind of emotions we will experience at any given time. If we realise we have moved away from dependency on God to a misplaced dependency on someone or something else, there is only one way back to right relationship with God, and that is through repentance.

Some years ago, God deeply challenged me through His words to the Church at Sardis in Revelation 3:1: 'I know your deeds; you have a reputation of being alive, but you are dead.' I was stricken because I knew the Holy Spirit was convicting me. On the outside my life looked all right – I was doing 'works'; I was involved in many things in the ministry. Through CWR I had 'a name', I looked 'alive'. But the Holy Spirit was telling me I was 'dead'.

In great anguish, I examined my life before God. Who was on the throne of my life? I had got more caught up in my work for God than with God Himself. I wept and repented, receiving God's forgiveness and cleansing. Praise Him! He sets us free from worshipping these wrong idols or pursuing these wrong goals, exposing our wrong thinking and choices. As these are corrected, our feelings fall in line as little ducks behind their mother on the water. It's crucial that we regularly examine our hearts before God, with a willingness to repent of our wrong and sinful strategies for living our lives independently of Him. This way of life needs to become our lifestyle.

Fiona told me, 'I realised that I often put my husband or family in place of God, and that I'd sought to satisfy my needs to be met in people and places, when only God could really fill them. In facing this, I've been able to grasp the incredible depth of God's love and grace for me and to turn afresh to Him, repent of my independence and offer myself fully again to Him. It has been incredibly liberating and redeeming.'[2]

The concepts of this chapter, together with exercises, are shared more fully in *Designed for Living* workbook.[3] And Selwyn Hughes in his book *Christ Empowered Living* also explains these concepts in greater depth and sets them in a broader context.[4]

Pause to reflect

As women, we are often governed by our emotions. We may put our loved ones or other things in place of God. Is the Holy Spirit showing you that you have allowed anything or anyone to take His place in your life? Identify any times when you may have been led by your emotions rather than focusing on Jesus. How might you graciously help others to a deeper dependence on God, rather than being led by their emotional state?

Greta, who organised the Designer Living seminar at Westminster Chapel, wrote afterwards, 'It was an "eye-opener" to have our patterns of behaviour revealed so clearly, and empowering to understand how to successfully handle life with its ups and downs – it is our choice. This gives us women a freedom and a responsibility.'[5]

Divine design

It is with joy I look to the future, seeking to live my life according to the divine design, knowing that this is where true fulfilment and satisfaction lie. I am committed to go on growing in God and to seize every opportunity to share these life-transforming truths with others. The deepening understanding that God designed me as a physical, longing, thinking, choosing and feeling being is the thing that empowers me more than any other in the life He has called me to live. Laying hold on this truth and applying it to your own life, will, I believe, do the same for you.[6]

NOTES
1. Sally's story appeared in the magazine *Christian Woman* (July/Aug 2000).
2. The testimonies of Fiona and Jenny, amongst others, may be found in CWR's *Designed for Living* workbook (Farnham: CWR, 2009).
3. Ibid.
4. *Christ Empowered Living*, Selwyn Hughes (Farnham: CWR, 2005).
5. 'Designer Living', *Empowering Women* (Surrey: CWR, 2005).
6. *Caring and Counselling* by Ron Kallmier (Farnham: CWR, 2011) is particularly helpful when seeking to apply these principles to assist other people.

HELPING HURTING PEOPLE
Rosalyn Derges

So, chosen by God for this new life of love, dress in the
wardrobe God picked out for you: compassion, kindness,
humility, quiet strength, discipline. Be even-tempered,
content with second place, quick to forgive an offense.
Forgive as quickly and completely as the Master forgave
you. And regardless of what else you put on, wear love.
It's your basic, all-purpose garment. Never be without it.

Colossians 3:12–14, *The Message*

Self-awareness

When I read these verses from Colossians, I ask myself how I measure
up. Some days I do not do too badly; on others I probably do not
do too well. I could sometimes do with a bigger dose of compassion
and kindness; as for discipline, it depends on what area of life we
are talking about. When it comes to humility and quiet strength,
my tendency is to let others know if the things I do have gone well
– it builds into my self-esteem. On the whole, these character traits
described in Colossians develop and grow as we move through life
and encounter different people, as well as experience different
situations. We are called to put on these characteristics as if we were
dressing up; and what we are dressing up for is to go out and meet

others with the best clothes we have. In this chapter we will look at how we might develop as helpers, rather than focus on individual needs and problems people experience. It is our character and skills that we will concentrate on.

Jesus moved towards people with kindness and compassion because He understood their pain. His most distinctive attribute, though, was love, which was why hurting people found it so easy to move towards Him and receive from Him. Jesus was completely self-aware. He knew the impact He had on different people. He wore these attributes with confidence and yet He remained humble with that quiet strength. Sometimes I know how I relate to others and how I 'come across', but there are times when I need friends to encourage me to overcome a blind spot. I suspect Paul was also encouraging the Colossians to become more aware of how they were dealing with one another; challenging them to love as they are loved by God. When God calls us to help hurting people, we must come from this place of being secure in knowing that we are loved, as well as deliberately growing in 'compassion, kindness, humility, gentleness and patience'.

Jesus was completely assured of the Father's love and was at ease with Himself; therefore, He was able to accept others, too, no matter where they were on their life's path. In my personal journey, I have found that being free to help other people requires me to accept myself and commit to allowing the Holy Spirit to change me by degrees. We do not have to strive to be perfect; we are perfected by God's love and Jesus' righteousness. If we want to reach out and help people, we need to create an accepting space for them to be who they are without judgement.

Pause to reflect

What characteristic would I like to see grow in my life? Do I allow my insecurities to become a barrier to others? How can I create a safe space for hurting people?

A good listener

> My dear brothers and sisters, take note of this: Everyone
> should be quick to listen, slow to speak ...
> > James 1:19, NIV 2011

One of the ways we can create a safe place for someone is to listen. Giving them the time to share their thoughts is powerful; it enables them to occupy a space that will help them to explore what is going on in their life. It is healing and releasing. When I was counselling people, the first session was an opportunity for the client to unfold their story. Often at the end of that session they would share how much they were helped just by being heard. When we listen, we communicate genuine care at a level deeper than 1,000 words can. How wonderful it is when someone gives us the gift of being listened to. We can feel accepted and quite special, as though what we have to say is important to another.

I am an extravert in the sense that I do not really know what I think until I have talked it out. So for me, when someone takes the time to listen, it enables me to process my thoughts and feelings. For some people, being able to express their pain, experiences and confusing thoughts helps them to work through and subsequently begin to understand what is going on for them. This is not a simple undertaking, this is multitasking. In order to really listen, we are using a number of skills.

Consider what you and I are doing when we listen. We are using our ears to hear not only words, but tone and speed of voice, as well as the emotion conveyed and language spoken. We use our eyes to watch for body language, facial expressions and to maintain eye contact. But we also listen with our soul; that is, our mind, heart, emotions and experience. And this is where the challenge comes; because we listen with who we are and from where we are, it is possible for us to get alongside others at a level that goes deep, enabling them to feel connected and heard. But it is also possible for us to allow our own thoughts, feelings and life experiences to inhibit our ability to help, because they get in the way. We may be filtering what the person says through our own preconceived ideas and expectations.

Suddenly, listening becomes complicated! But we are talking about helping hurting people, and we need to come to this with a desire to see healing taking place in that person, and not bring our own agenda into the process. We might need to check out what is going on inside of us and ask ourselves if there are any negative or unhelpful attitudes reverberating within us. It can also be difficult to give ourselves fully to listening if we are tired or there are pressures in our own lives.

We also listen to others with our spirit. God has enabled us to be guided by and filled with His Spirit so that when we spend time with others, He is there too. The Spirit equips us with discernment and an awareness that will help us to tune in to the deeper things going on within a person. It is good to ask God to go with us into these situations so that we can be confident of a helper who knows everything there is to know. This requires us to spend time with Him and to expect Him to be involved in the healing of someone who is in need of a touch from a God who is compassionate and kind.

Pause to reflect

As you listen to others, become aware of the skills you are using. Ask God to enhance those skills and develop others within you. Do you tend to bring your own issues into the conversation? Develop your spiritual ears to discern the needs at a deeper level.

Empathy

Consider for a moment someone with whom you feel safe, and creates that space for you to feel heard. What characteristics do they possess? The chances are that one you will identify will be empathy. This is the quality that really enfolds us in a safe place, and one that ensures us of a heart that is ready to give us what we need when we are hurting.

When I am hurting, I need someone who will somehow convey that they understand, without saying, 'I know just how you feel'. My ideal helper will let me pour out the words without trying to rescue me or tell me what to do. They will respond so that I know they have heard me and will pick up on the important things I am saying. I don't want pity or sympathy, but I desperately need empathy. In Ephesians we are encouraged to 'Be kind and compassionate to one another' (Eph. 4:32) and 'live a life of love' (Eph 5:2). This kind of empathy implies that we need to consider what sort of help this person really needs.

Sometimes a cup of coffee and a chat is just what is required. I have a friend who is great at this kind of ministry. She asks God to bring people across her path so she can invite them out just at the right time for them to experience care. She has some amazing encounters which can lead to a longer-term pastoral relationship. Empathy enables us to recognise when someone needs to unload for a one-off session, or if they need something that will require more time. Empathy embodies qualities such as trust, kindness, giving time, honesty and many more.

In order to show empathy, we can respond in such a way as to let the person know we care. Often when someone is in pain they find it difficult to express themselves, and so we need to create the kind of atmosphere where they are able to go slowly and experience periods of silence without feeling uncomfortable. We need to develop the skill of handling silence, too. Silence can allow thoughts to develop, what you have shared to sink in, emotions to be felt and, of course, God to speak. Often reflecting back the words the person has spoken can enable them to know they have been heard, as well as experiencing them in a different way. I have experienced situations where people have poured out their thoughts and have no idea what they have said. When I have reflected back their own words, it is as if they have heard them for the first time. This can be empowering for them as they then begin to own their thoughts and feelings.

At times it can be difficult to understand how the person is facing their situation, and we need to clarify what they have said. Language and intention can be misinterpreted if we don't make clear what we have heard. In the case of problems in relationships, for example, what one person has said can so easily be misunderstood by the other through negative feelings. Checking out what we have heard can bring an appreciation of what life looks like for that person.

What we are doing here is building a relationship that becomes secure and one where, if we do need to go deeper, we can be used by the Spirit to facilitate restoration towards a sense of peace and hope. We can begin to reflect back not only words but feelings expressed and not expressed. Sometimes we discern emotions that are not easily spoken, and we can tentatively share what we are sensing. This can often only be done when that trust is created through empathic responses. We might also reflect back body language to check out how they might be experiencing the process at that time.

In order to improve our empathy skills we need to return to self-awareness: we must be in touch with our own feelings. Emotions can take us by surprise at times; they act as an indicator that something is not quite right within. I have become aware that my feelings can lead me into negative thinking and behaviours that challenge my maturity. One helpful mantra I have developed to check out my emotions is this:

- What am I feeling?
- Why am I feeling it?
- What am I going to do about it?

Another way to improve empathy is to ask God to deepen our ability. He has an interest in the growth and development of our capacity to help others, and we need to recognise He wants to be involved. In our concern for others, we can often rush the process so they stop feeling the hurt; sometimes we need to slow things down by listening to the Spirit as they are sharing. Giving ourselves time to think enhances our aptitude to empathise as well as tune in to how the person is experiencing life.

Pause to reflect

In what ways can I improve my empathy skills? Do I allow time for others to think, or feel I have to come up with the answer? Am I comfortable with clarifying, or do I think I know what they mean?

Equipped by God

> This is my life work: helping people understand and respond to this Message. It came as a sheer gift to me, a real surprise, God handling all the details. When it came to presenting the Message to people who had no background in God's way, I was the least qualified of any of the available Christians. God saw to it that I was *equipped*, but you can be sure that it had nothing to do with my natural abilities.
>
> Eph. 3:7–8, The Message, my italics

Paul is entirely confident that God equipped him for his mission, and He will equip us for ours. We can sometimes feel out of our depth, but God has clearly given us everything we need to help others. The greatest gift we can offer is to be ourselves. We are not going to know all the answers, nor are we going to be able to rescue people from their pain; only God can do that in reality. But God can provide us with what we need in order to serve one another. In other words, we don't know all the answers, but we know a Man who does! If we come into pastoral situations with the belief that we are chosen to get alongside hurting people, then we can begin to see that, if we ask Him, God will give us an ability to see things through His eyes. In his book *The Contemplative Pastor*, Eugene Peterson encourages us to ask ourselves this question: 'How many people have you listened to in Christ this week?'[1]

That phrase 'in Christ' means we are not in this alone. It is Christ who gives us what we need to reach out and help. Suddenly the responsibility is God's and not ours. What a relief! Such a burden lifted. This kind of prayerful attitude is such a powerful tool in the hand and heart of the listener. And this is our conclusion.

We can try to do all of the above in our own strength, or we do it hand in hand with God through the power of His Spirit. The burden of a person's healing lies with their Creator, but He chooses to use us to facilitate part of the process. He does not want us to bring solutions to the problems, but He wants to bring a resolution to the deep longings of the heart. He does not want people patched up with a temporary good feeling, but redeemed and made whole by His love, which is as real in the pain as it is when the pain is relieved.

Pause to reflect

You might like to say the following prayer:

> Loving Lord, You long for your children to come and sit at Your feet and listen to Your voice. Speak into our hearts now. Increase our ability to create a safe place for those who are hurting. May we get alongside each one in the way they need so they experience healing from Your hand. Teach us how to see what You are doing in the lives of individuals so we don't get in the way, but are able to help so that restoration can be brought into their hearts, minds and spirits. We pray for opportunity and the wisdom to use the gifts You have given to bring love and compassion, hope and peace. Give us listening ears and hearts, quiet spirits, and the knowledge that You are walking beside us every step of the way. For Your glory Lord, Amen.

NOTE

1. Eugene Peterson, *The Contemplative Pastor* (Grand Rapids, MI: William B. Eerdmans Publishing Co., 1993).

THE POWER OF COMMUNICATION

Lynn Penson

What is communication? Communicating can be thought of as the passing on of thoughts and ideas from one person to another. However, this is a one-way process; good communication goes beyond this. It has been defined as:

> The exchange of thoughts, messages, or information as by speech, signals, writing, or behaviour.[1]

or

> A two-way process of reaching mutual understanding, in which participants not only exchange (encode-decode) information but also create and share meaning.[2]

I particularly like this latter definition. It seems to be rich in the value it puts on the mutuality of the process, and suggests something very meaningful about the relationship that results when we communicate well. In short, good communication is the key to healthy relationships. Conversely, poor communication is a cause of the breakdown of good relationships.

Pause to reflect

When someone is communicating with you, whether they are speaking to you as an individual or to you as part of a large group, what do you find
   a) effective and helpful?
   b) ineffective and unhelpful?
Jot down any thoughts.

When we are in a position of ministering to other women (or men or children), we are not only communicating thoughts or information, we are also communicating attitudes. As we talk to someone we should ask ourselves, 'Does this person feel respected and valued by the way I am communicating?' Or, 'Do they feel I am not interested, and in a rush to get on to the next conversation or activity?'

Communication skills

The Greek sage and Stoic philosopher Epictetus wisely said, 'We have two ears and one mouth so that we can listen twice as much as we speak.' Listening is a message in itself; when we listen well, we are communicating to the person speaking that what they have to say is important to us, and for many people that will mean that they will feel valued for themselves.

Sydney Harris said that the two words *information* and *communication* 'are often used interchangeably, but they signify quite different things. Information is giving out: communication is getting through.' I have found the Shannon–Weaver communication model[3] a useful tool to keep in mind when speaking to others, whether a group of people, or in a one-to-one situation. It reminds us that good communication is not just about what I say as the communicator, but about the way it is heard and received. It is 'getting through' that is important, and that will be determined by a number of factors. I have drawn on this model but adapted it for our purposes in this chapter.

The message

What is it that we want to communicate to others? Whether we are leading a study group, preaching a sermon or talking one-to-one, we need to be clear about what we are saying. If we are discussing a Bible passage, have we done our homework and worked to understand it as best we can? Are we careful to be accurate, and not to give inappropriate advice in a pastoral situation?

It is also helpful to consider carefully the purpose of our message. Is it to inform, to educate, to inspire, to encourage, or to motivate for action? Knowing what our objective is, and keeping this in the forefront of our mind will help us to keep our focus clear and prevent us going 'off track'. Our purpose will shape what we say and how we say it.

The communicator

We do not need a theology degree to be able to teach from Scripture, but if we are going to teach others, we do need to recognise the importance of being informed and equipped as well as possible by good research, which may come through personal reading or attending training courses. If we are teaching God's Word, then we must be continual students of Scripture, and be well clued-up about what is going on in the world around us.

We need to consider what our lives might be saying to our listeners. How do we prepare ourselves, not just the message? Three questions we might want to ask:

1. Have we spent time listening to God before we speak to others?
Are we able to convey to people something of God Himself, rather than conveying ourselves? There is a place for sharing ourselves, and telling our personal story can be a great encouragement to others when done with honesty and thoughtfulness, but the prime purpose must be to point people to God.

2. 'What do I believe about myself, my audience and my message?' (Three questions in one.)
Finding our personal security in God will help us to manage all

three in a more positive way, otherwise we may find ourselves crippled with anxiety. For a number of years, I felt ill every Thursday morning. It was the day that I was going to be lecturing Bible college students in subjects including church history, ethics, and communication skills. Why was I so anxious? I was concerned about so many things. What if the students didn't like me? What if they asked a question I didn't have an answer for? What if I got something wrong or went blank or forgot something important? What if my colleagues thought I was not good at my job? I did face some problems as a female Bible college lecturer back in the early 1990s, but God had plans for me. Coming to a transformational place involved finding my security, self-worth and significance in Christ. As a result, I found I was able to rise above those self-doubts, although there were still times I needed to give myself a good talking to; but I was no longer at the mercy of my need to find approval from anyone and everyone. Being able to both respect and not feel intimidated by the people listening was an important feature of being able to speak with confidence. I continued to work hard to present my material in a thorough and accessible way, but was able to feel enthused and confident in what I was teaching.

3. Are we personally living out what we teach others? Do we teach and encourage others with integrity?

Reflect on these questions. When you last spoke to, or led, a group, were you aware of your beliefs about yourself, your message and the people you were with? Is there something that you need to think more about before you speak or lead again?

The communication method

Auditory, visual, tactile communication. If we are speaking to a small or large group, then the spoken word is probably going to be our preferred method of communication. However, we can use other ways of helping our message to be passed on effectively. Those technical wizards among us may be able to use PowerPoint if addressing a larger group, but that is by no means the only, or even the best, way of providing extra stimulation. The use of music, pictures, symbols or activities will all enhance the message. Bearing in mind that some people prefer to learn by listening (auditory), others by seeing (visual), and yet others by doing (kinaesthetic/tactile), it is helpful to incorporate a range of communication methods. Even in one-to-one situations, the use of pictures or some form of activity can be helpful.

Pause to reflect

What do you find most helpful when learning – what you see, what you hear, what you do? Do you tend to keep to this method when speaking to others, or do you try to use a variety of methods?

Communicating by writing. Writing is an art that often seems lost, except in the shortened version of texting or emailing. In our marriage and preparation for marriage courses at Waverley, we set aside time for couples to write to one another. For many this is a novel experience, but it becomes a very meaningful one. We should never underestimate the effectiveness of sending written words of encouragement to others, even if we meet up with them regularly.

Non-verbal communication. We need to remember that as we communicate, it is not only the words that are important, but also the non-verbal parts.

Professor Mehrabian's research led to a formula which applies to the communication of feelings and attitudes by the spoken word. He said that 7 per cent of a message pertaining to feelings and attitudes is in the words spoken, 38 per cent is in the way the words are said, and 55 per cent is in the body language. In other words, people are not just listening to the words, but also to the way we say them. While words are powerful, the way we say them is even more so. Try telling someone you love them using an angry voice, or while looking at your watch, or gazing out of the window. What are those words going to mean to the person hearing them? Do they go away knowing that they are absolutely loved? I suggest that is highly unlikely.

It is a good thing for us to ask ourselves how we rate on our eye contact, facial expressions, the way we stand or sit, our tone and pace of speaking. Alternatively, ask a friend who will be honest. We can improve these with some thought, welcoming other people's comments and practising in front of a mirror.

Our body language will, in part, be affected by how we feel about ourselves. If we feel anxious or embarrassed we will often show it until we find ways of dealing with those emotional instincts. If we are struggling with these things it is likely to impact others, and so we need to find ways to deal with them.

Verbal communication. While Professor Mehrabian attributed only 7 per cent of a message, relating to feeling and attitudes, to the words used, we also know that words are powerful and we need to recognise this in all our conversations. The book of Proverbs has a great deal to say on the power of words: 'The tongue has the power of life and death' (Prov. 18:21), 'The tongue that brings healing is a tree of life, but a deceitful tongue crushes the spirit' (Prov. 15:4).

James, in his New Testament letter, writes about the power of words, which can be like dangerous sparks that can set a whole forest on fire (see James 3:5). For some of us, the words are out of our mouths before we have really thought about them and decided whether they should be said or held back. We need to weigh up our words and the impact they will have on the people receiving them. The old adage of counting to ten before saying anything is a wise one on many occasions, but how many of us are disciplined enough to really take time to think through what we are about to say before verbalising it? I have found myself in difficult situations by not carefully considering the effect my words might have on the listener.

'Noise'

In order for what we say to be fully heard, we need to consider the distractions that could prevent our message from hitting its target. This we call 'noise'.

Look back at your response to the question about what you find unhelpful when people are communicating. Often these things come into a category that includes both internal and external noise.

It might be actual noise that creates a barrier – the sound of machinery drowning out your words, microphone failure, the cry of a baby; but it could also be other distractions – being too hot or too cold to be able to concentrate, poor lighting, uncomfortable seating. The distracting mannerisms of a speaker might mean that the message gets lost. Other noise factors include problems with understanding a strong accent or the vocabulary used, which might be too difficult or too new. Our tone of voice and body language are also relevant here.

More difficult to spot immediately is internal noise. The barrier that is created by differences in culture and attitudes can lead to misunderstanding or resentment, ultimately resulting in the person listening 'switching off'.

If we are to communicate well, we need to provide a good and helpful environment so that people are able to listen without obvious distraction. This applies whether we are working with a large group or having a conversation with one other. We also need to consider our own attitudes to people who are different from us, whether that is in terms of personality, status, physical differences or culture. Checking out prejudices which might affect the way we relate to others may be uncomfortable, but will help us to understand how other people could be receiving what we say.

Hearing and receiving the message

As communicators, we need to ensure that the message gets through by being heard and understood, and with as little interference from distracting noises as possible.

Feedback

In order to ensure that our communication has been heard and understood accurately, we should seek feedback wherever possible. This provides the opportunity for ongoing communication between two people or with a group. It may be formal, or the asking of an open question.

Communicating to a crowd

If you are not used to public speaking, it can be very daunting to find yourself addressing a large group. There is no substitute for doing this regularly to boost your confidence levels, providing you have at least some of the basic skills in place. However, here are some confidence boosters for communicators finding themselves anxious in such a situation.

1. Prepare well. There is probably nothing that will sap confidence more than speaking without sufficient preparation. There should be no excuse for poor preparation, especially if you are taking on the responsibility of sharing something of God's truth with others.
2. Be particularly thoroughly rehearsed and confident in your opening sentences, and endings.
3. Arrive early and check out the room and equipment, especially if you are not familiar with the location. If you are using an adjustable lectern, ensure it is set at the correct height. Have a soundcheck if you are using a microphone.
4. Dress comfortably for yourself and your audience. Being under- or overdressed can create a barrier with your audience, though one that can always be overcome.
5. Smile! Look! Engage your audience and get a response as early as possible – laughter is a great icebreaker if used well and appropriately.
6. People usually like to know something about you as a person, so introduce yourself in a straightforward way.
7. Look out for friendly faces. Allow their smiles to encourage you, but do not give them all your attention. Allow your eyes to move over the entire group.
8. Breathe deeply before you begin. This opens up your air passages, and gives a bold start for your voice. It also helps to relax you.
9. Be clear about your aim and what you want to achieve.
10. Use audio and visual aids wherever appropriate and possible, but only use those that you are confident in using, and be careful not to overuse them. Avoid 'death by PowerPoint'. Keep such

aids simple and clear. Don't talk to the screen if using one, and remember that the best audio visual aid should be you!

11. Pray – remember that you are the messenger, but the message is God's.

Communication in smaller groups

The effective leading of a small group does not happen by chance. I believe that opportunity to interact is useful in the largest of groups, but is particularly important in smaller groups; yet it is not always easy to manage. If you have led groups for a long time, you will probably have met those people who talk too much, want to give advice, throw in distractions or red herrings, disagree with everything and everyone, talk over others, or never contribute. And sometimes a group as a whole might be silent, or impossible to quieten down.

As a leader of the group, it is important to have a clear aim in mind, while being prepared to be flexible when the need arises. You will need to take responsibility so that one person does not dominate or dampen the discussion. You may have to be direct, suggesting that others also be given the opportunity to share their views. You might also need to be firm in dealing with irrelevant or unhelpful questions so that the main purpose of the conversation does not get hijacked.

One way to encourage everyone to participate is to put people into smaller groups to discuss a particular question. In some situations, giving people permission not to contribute might help them feel more able to attend, until a time when they are confident enough to participate.

When working with people, do so with consideration and graciousness, and remember that maintaining a healthy balanced group will require ensuring that one person does not dominate discussion.

Who is it for?

One of the reasons I found the communication model referred to earlier useful was because it reminded me that communicating is not just about me and my message, but is about the people receiving it. While it is vital to prepare yourself and what you are going to say, your effectiveness is going to be limited if you have not considered the people who will hear you. I can speak as loudly and enthusiastically as is possible, but if they are not fully hearing and understanding, my best efforts will be in vain. This is why I find it helpful to know something about the people I am going to speak to so that I can pray, not just for myself but for them. It is in considering the hearer, their comfort and their needs, that we can go beyond selfish motives to 'create and share meaning' and to truly minister to them.

NOTES
1. www.thefreedictionary.com
2. www.businessdictionary.com/definition/communication.html
3. Shannon-Weaver communication model:
    http://members.westnet.com.au

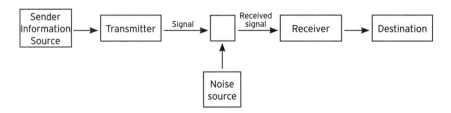

LEADING GROUPS AND RUNNING EVENTS

Jane Follett

The church I attend and love is Christ the King which stands next to a large housing estate on the edge of Kettering. Built in the 1980s, it is the only church serving the Ise Lodge estate and the main provider of youth work, mums and tots and older people's groups, and children's clubs. Our church vision is 'Growing Together: Deeper in Discipleship; Closer in Friendship; Further in Partnership – Growing Relevant Relationships'.

In 2005 I was asked by the vicar, Steve Bennoy, to develop women's ministry at church in line with our church vision. With Steve's wise advice, and the encouragement and the help of many women, a thriving new ministry area has grown with a variety of activities.

The aim of this chapter is to offer some encouragement and guidance in the whole area of leading groups and running events.

Why?

Some initial questions and comments to consider are:
- Is there a perceived need for an event to bring women together, or to reach women in the community?
- Do you feel the Lord is prompting you to start a particular group, or have you been asked to lead an existing one? Asking the question, 'Why am I doing this?' will help you to consider such

things as: Is this the Holy Spirit's prompting? Is it our church vision? Is the reason a result of a groundswell of opinion, or a straightforward request from leadership? You need to know that if you are going to invest time and effort, there is a need, and that the Lord is calling you to meet it. Tread gently if there are existing groups and, if possible, join in and serve there first.

- If your church leadership has not asked you to specifically take on a role in this area of ministry, have you spoken to your vicar or minister first to make sure that you are working under their authority and with their blessing?

- If your church has a vision statement, work within that to enhance and complement what is being done across the whole church: 'Now you are the body of Christ, and each one of you is a part of it' (1 Cor. 12: 27).

- Who is the event or group for? Although it may well be open to all women, there may be a particular group in church that has a need that is pressing or not met in other areas of church life. Groups might focus around mums with young children who are too tired for evening meetings, single mums, single working women, or women with long-term health problems, empty-nesters, the newly retired, and the elderly. You can't organise things for them separately, but it is worth bearing in mind those groups that you may feel need some extra encouragement. It is important to take seriously the day, times and venue that would work best.

- If you have a well-established women's ministry programme, you can probably put on an event for an age-specific group without the others feeling left out, but if you are only just starting, it is probably helpful to do something that will appeal to most women.

Pause to reflect

Consider the questions and comments above. Has anything really spoken to your heart? Are there any you need to bring to the Lord right now?

Before any planning, take time to pray and seek the Lord for His heart. Ask Him to bring women alongside you whom He is also stirring up to share the vision and the work. Once you have a clear mandate to organise a group or event, it's time to start meeting those women whom you have asked the Lord to send.

Starting off

When I was asked to develop and lead this ministry area, I first joined the existing women's Bible study group, 'Manna'. I had a great couple of years getting to know the women there before I was asked to join the leadership team. God's timing was perfect, and He has brought about many changes to this group that have been a huge blessing. It has not been without some upheaval but has been done with unity. The Manna group now has about sixty regular members ranging from twenty to eighty years, a teaching team, worship, hospitality, prayer ministry, testimony, a Christianity Explored[1] group, and a crèche. It continues to be a pool of deep, life-giving spiritual refreshment where women meet with Jesus. It is building up women, fostering nurturing relationships between them, and also giving a place where women can grow and develop their gifting. Relationships are at the heart of this ministry area. Getting to know women is key. Start meeting up with women across the Church and getting to know them better – their gifting, their experience, their pain and their passions. Get into the habit of praying with each woman you meet. It doesn't need to be complicated or deep.

When?

When I started doing women's ministry, I asked for a copy of the long-term church calendar to provide an overview of what was happening. Thinking of the church vision, 'Deeper in Discipleship, Closer in Friendship and Further in Partnership' and of the rhythm of the church year, I could start to plan groups and events that complemented what was happening and addressed discipleship, encouraged friendship and reached out to the community. For example, the end of November has proved to be a good time for a retreat and for our Creative Advent evening event. Similarly, early June has been a good time for our summer retreat. January is a dismal month for many, so our conference is on the last Saturday, with December kept free of any planning. There is much to be said for establishing some key dates in the church diary, as we have found women then keep that date free from year to year and look forward to those special times. For our bi-term Coffee and Croissant mornings, we have found that a 9.30am start and 11.30am finish gives women a chance to drop in for a leisurely breakfast while not spending too much time away from home. Evening events need to allow women to travel home from work and/or get their children to bed, and finish in time to get to bed at a reasonable hour. We only have evening events during the week so as not to disrupt family life, and plan well in advance, consulting with any home groups that meet on that night.

What?

One of the ways that our small Bible study meetings within our large Manna group have deepened in friendship is through eating together and spending time outside of our usual Tuesday morning setting. If you belong to a small group, why not start just where you are; invite the other women for a meal, or go out together for a coffee, or a visit to the cinema or theatre?

Events
Once you are sure of why, for whom and when you want to run an event, you need to work with a team of women who are sharing the vision for this.

Planning tips:
- Have as few meetings and as tight a 'who does what' list as possible. It helps if someone can take notes and email everyone afterwards so that people are clear about what they need to do, and deadlines.
- Make things as beautiful and personal as possible, appealing to all the senses, such as fresh flowers, hand cream and nice

soap in the loos, pretty tablecloths, tea lights, proper coffee, and special biscuits.

- Publicity: Pretty, clear and inviting. Find someone with graphic design skills to do this. Give it out in good time with a smile and 'We'd love you to come!'
- Price-wise, try to keep it as accessible as possible. Maybe charge enough so that you can give a few tickets to those who couldn't afford to come otherwise.
- Think about the shyest women who might come, and think through what would help them chat with others: Icebreakers, table-top quizzes, table hosts, 'meet and greeters' who are there to specifically watch out for those on their own and include them and introduce them to others.
- Plan to have help with all practical tasks on the day/evening, so you are ready to chat rather than rushing about doing last-minute jobs. Maybe some men would come and do this. We have a brilliant men's team who help at our Women's Conference, and also teenage stewards and greeters.

All these things will help women feel welcome and more likely to want to come again.

Pause to reflect

What kind of events might work in your church? What team might the Lord be calling you to put together? You might like to call a friend to begin to pray through some of the suggestions above.

Ideas for events

Food and drink are always a great asset to any event, so think about what and where this should be included. You could include a short testimony if you felt it would be appropriate. Invite women to bring their mums, neighbours, teenage daughters, friends and colleagues.

Craft-based events appeal to lots of women. It's best if this is linked to the theme of the evening.

Beading evening. Many women enjoy beading; ask their advice, and order lots of beautiful beads, charging accordingly. You can use very thin waxed thread, a metre per person, and then thread random beads onto it – recycled are great – tying a knot before and after. When it's finished, the two loose ends are popped one over the other and hang in front.

Creative Advent. Invite some 'crafty' people to prepare a Christmassy item to make that takes about forty-five minutes, set up on tables with all materials at the ready. They could also sell some of their own crafts. When the women arrive, they can wander round and look at the different items, and choose what they would like to make. Warn people when you are getting near to the end of the session, so you can all finish on time. For the last few years we have had a special moment when we all light a candle, turn the lights out and hold someone up to God in our thoughts and prayers. (Our visitors may not come to church, so we want to make such a moment relevant and uncringy.) Alternatively you could plan *Advent wreath-making.* The smell of evergreen plants is wonderful, especially when complemented by mince pies and punch.

Learn a specific craft. Head into your local art gallery or library or look on the internet to find out about local specialists who will come and teach a craft. (Maybe you already have someone at your church who is an expert.)

Social events

Colour and swapping evening: Track down a colour consultant and discuss how all women can be involved so that it is an interactive, fun evening. Ask women to bring a scarf, and possibly some beads they no longer want, to swap after they've found out what colour suits them.

Antiques Roadshow: Track down a local expert to talk about items brought in by the group; may particularly appeal to the older ladies.

Gardeners' Question Time: We invited four people, including the owner of our local family-run garden centre, a local radio garden expert and two 'home-grown' experts from church, and proceeded as in the Radio Four programme. It was very popular and great fun.

Women's Breakfasts: We have coffee and croissants, but bacon sandwiches would be great too! Have a discussion during the second hour, or invite one of your own women to share a testimony.

Other events
Retreat days

You could start by taking others on an organised retreat, but then plan your own, which is cheaper; also, you can tailor it to suit your women's needs. Find an inexpensive retreat or conference centre not too far away. We invite a speaker who only speaks for about ten minutes two or three times during the day. The rest of the time is spent in worship which begins and ends the day, and periods of quiet between talks, where we read and meditate on/pray through scriptures suggested by the retreat leader.[2]

Day conference

A conference needs a lot of prayer and planning. I have prayed about the theme and booked our speaker and venue eighteen months before the January conference, and though it can be done in less time, it is best to plan well in advance if you want a particular speaker and venue. The team has a whole day of prayer and seeking God before planning. The artwork for promotions, tickets and workshop leaders are also organised well in advance.

Over the years I've written job descriptions for the team roles, and we now have: treasurer, administrator, hospitality, prayer (overseeing prayer room and prayer ministry), seminar coordinator, worship leaders and conference organiser.

We try to make the whole day beautiful for the women who come, with fresh flowers, goody bags, hand massage, special biscuits and lots of people to greet and look after them. We are hugely blessed by our wonderful team of male helpers, and also sixth form students who wear special 'Steward' T-shirts. The seminars and workshops have ranged from bongo drumming to contemplative prayer, with themes such as depression, dementia and youth.

I felt the conference (and myself) needed some godly, wise, experienced women who would pray for us, and to whom we could turn for advice. It is a delight to have them watching over us.

The conference is now open to women from all churches in the area, and in 2012, our third 'open' year, we had women from nearly sixty churches attending. The sense of the Lord's blessing on the women and His delight at the unity was very real.

A key to running a conference is to start small and simple, and allow it to grow and develop as you grow in confidence as the Lord leads. You may like to partner with CWR's women's regional team to help you in your first event.[3]

Organising groups

Organising a group is a big commitment. You need to be sure that there is a need and that you have the team to support it and enable it to flourish without it becoming a drain on anyone.

Starting with a limited time span might be a good idea. We have run a Women's Lent group in the past, and some young women did CWR's 'How to be a Secure Woman'[4] course.

Here are some thoughts based on the groups I run.

Community group

The Lord clearly led me to run a community and church group for women. Six years have passed since the WEFT group started. (Why 'WEFT'? It stands for 'Women Enjoying Friendship Together' – but the key idea is in a weaving context; weft is the horizontal threads that are woven in and out of the framework of warp threads. The framework is like Jesus, the Weaver – the Holy Spirit weaving our lives together to make something beautiful to bless the Lord and us.)

Most weeks we have three crafts to choose from, and finish with a 'Thought for the Evening'. But we have done many other things, including choral speaking (like a choir but using the spoken word – usually to speak poetry – sometimes one voice, small groups or all together), an owl evening – when seventeen owls visited – followed by four weeks making owl-related things, a barbecue and campfire at a nearby Scout centre in a wood, with singing and marshmallows, film nights with popcorn, memory evenings, netball, an exercise group, games and meals together. We have met in schools and churches. We have two add-on groups – one helps women who are trying to control their eating, and is run by two nurses, and the other is a book group.

We started WEFT for women from church only for the first half term. This allowed us to establish the group, so that when we opened it to the community, they knew that things such as 'Thought for the Evening' were part of the programme. We have found that most women are happy to ask for prayer for others; this remains a key part of the evening, and one which we all value.

We have not advertised the group, but have let it grow by word of mouth. About twenty-five women come most weeks, with a good mix from church and non-church backgrounds. We have been able to support women who are bereaved, divorced, lonely, isolated, pressured by family demands, illness and depression, but WEFT always has a buzz of laughter, chatter, and a sense of purpose. As one woman writes, 'The fellowship of the other ladies is something I look forward to all week. If I have a problem there is always a listening ear and support available.' And from another lady, 'the friendship and company ... have helped me through some very difficult times.'

In a gentle way we try to point people to Jesus, and at the end of each term we have a service in a nearby village church. We may sing, and there are items around the church to touch or look at, things to take away, candles to light, and space to be quiet, to write a prayer request or 'thank you'. These are always special times when the Lord touches women and draws them closer to Himself.

Bible study group

We start promptly and include worship, teaching, and Bible study and prayer. As we have grown, we now work like a 'roots group'; people join a group where they know someone, and the group grows until it is too big when, in theory, it splits into two.

We have found it helpful to have a team that plans the studies, usually based on a 'Lifebuilder'[5] book, but prepared in such a way that the study does not become too school-like or too long.

As a team we plan for a balance over the year with a DVD course, Bible studies based on a book, then maybe a theme-based study. We try to have a balance between Old Testament and New Testament teaching. The Holy Spirit often brings deep things to the surface, and last year we started to offer prayer ministry sessions during the morning. These have been very helpful for some of the women, and they welcome them being at a time when their children can be safely left in the crèche.

Pause to reflect

Have you any particular groups of women in your church who have a real need that is not being met? What might the Lord be calling you to do for them?

Raising up leaders

Our church runs a CPAS 'Growing Leaders' course[6], and it has been great in refining the work that the Holy Spirit has begun. Women have been growing into leadership through a variety of ways within women's ministry. Looking back, it is amazing the variety of women involved in the teams, and how they have grown through these.

When Claire and I first met, she was expecting her second baby; five years later, she has four little ones and is an extremely busy wife and mum. I knew Claire loved digging deep into Scripture and, with a Master's degree in philosophy, she clearly loved words and ideas. The first time Claire gave a talk, it was like watching an amazing athlete run for the first time; this was what Claire was created for. She now heads up all our teaching and has started to preach in our main church services.

Janet and Dani lead 'Christianity Explored' and 'Discipleship Explored'[7] groups, and Dani also comes to WEFT. Janet joined Christ the King about three years ago, when she and her husband, John, moved near Kettering. Following John's death, and her own health problems, Janet started coming to Manna. In her eighties, and with a life-time of Christian ministry with her husband, she has been a huge blessing to us and has been key in raising up Dani as a leader. There is much informal mentoring like this going on, as well as formal mentoring through 'Growing Leaders', and is an area we would like to develop.

Elsa and Marcia have been able to exercise their prophetic gifting in prayer ministry, one-to-one encouragement, and in developing worship at our conferences. Others have started to lead worship, three are starting a group with women who have come out of abusive relationships, and one is training to be a vicar.

After many years' teaching in a special unit, family illness, caring for elderly parents, supporting children and grandchildren, Val felt on the edge of church life and she knew others felt the same. Val and I have known each other for a long time, but in the last two years we have grown closer and I have turned to her for advice and wisdom. Val decided to take slightly early retirement to spend more time with her husband, and has driven events that attract older women, as well as women of her daughter's generation. Because of Val's long-established relationships, women have wanted to come along to the Book Club, Coffee and Croissant mornings and social events she organises. She has also reached out to new women at church and drawn them into the circle of love.

Karen is Val's daughter. She works long unsocial hours as a nurse practitioner, and although she knows many women at church, can't get to a weekly group and misses seeing other mums at the school gate. One-off social events have been great for Karen and the Lord has met with her powerfully at the conferences.

Deeper, closer, further

I think the most important thing that women's ministry events and groups can offer a church are opportunities for women to develop relevant relationships – whether that's meeting new people within church, or strengthening existing friendships and reaching out to include others. As we have reached further into our community, others have been touched by the love of Jesus expressed in these events or at WEFT. Through the weekly Manna Bible group, retreats and annual conferences, women meet with Jesus in different ways, and through the work of the Holy Spirit, grow in maturity.[8]

Pause to reflect

Reflect on this scripture, and thank God for inspiration and encouragement:

... blessed are those who trust in the LORD and have made the LORD their hope and confidence. They are like trees planted along a riverbank, with roots that reach deep into the water. Such trees are not bothered by the heat or worried by long months of drought. Their leaves stay green, and they never stop producing fruit.

Jer. 17:7–8, NLT

NOTES

1. *Christianity Explored* is a seven-session course on DVD and with supporting workbook and leaders' guides that helps people explore the basic of the Christian faith through Mark's Gospel. We have found this ideal as women are then introduced to the idea of studying the Bible and can then move on to *Discipleship Explored*, see www.christianityexplored.org and www.discipleshipexplored.org

2. The Retreat Association. For lists of retreats and information on leading a retreat, see: www.retreats.org

3. See details of our conference at www.ctk.org.uk; click on women's conference.

4. Jeannette Barwick, *How to be a Secure Woman* (Farnham: CWR, 2005). This is also run as a day's seminar.

5. Lifebuilder Bible Studies are a Scripture Union resource that we have used a lot and found very good. See www.scriptureunion.org Alternatively CWR has an extensive range of Bible Study Guides.

6. The CPAS 'Growing Leaders' course focuses on developing leaders across the life of the Church, and provides practical resources for running a leadership development process over a year. See www.cpas.org.uk/church-resources/growing-leaders-suite

7. See end note 1.

8. Other useful links: Restored: This is an international Christian alliance working to transform relationships and end violence against women. www.restoredrelationships.org; Activate: This organisation has great ideas for events and an annual weekend conference. It used to be called Christian Viewpoint for Women: www.activateyourlife.org.uk; *Woman Alive* magazine is full of inspiring stories and each month there are ideas for events or groups plus excellent teaching. You can also read these on their website. See www.womanalive.co.uk

Small group resources: Know your Bible. This organisation has good study guides that include studies for during the week. It also organises regional conferences. Very structured and good for small groups especially if you are just starting a group. See www.knowyourbible.org.uk

The Road to Maturity: a six-week DVD course with booklets by Mary Pytches is a New Wine resource that was excellent. See www.new-wine.org

7 Laws for Life: a seven-week DVD course, with Selwyn Hughes teaching. We found it engaging and challenging and would highly recommend. See www.cwr.org.uk

ONE-YEAR READING PLAN WITH BIBLE TEXT

THE

REVEALING
GOD'S COVENANT PLAN
FOR EVERYONE

STORY

Transforming lives

Courses and seminars

Publishing and new media

Conference facilities

CWR Applying God's Word
to everyday life and relationships

CWR, Waverley Abbey House,
Waverley Lane, Farnham,
Surrey GU9 8EP, UK

Telephone: +44 (0)1252 784700
Email: info@cwr.org.uk
Website: www.cwr.org.uk

Registered Charity No 294387
Company Registration No 1990308

CWR's vision is to enable people to experience personal transformation through applying God's Word to their lives and relationships.

Our Bible-based training and resources help people around the world to:
• Grow in their walk with God
• Understand and apply Scripture to their lives
• Resource themselves and their church
• Develop pastoral care and counselling skills
• Train for leadership
• Strengthen relationships, marriage and family life and much more.

Our insightful writers provide daily Bible-reading notes and other resources for all ages, and our experienced course designers and presenters have gained an international reputation for excellence and effectiveness.

CWR's Training and Conference Centre in Surrey, England, provides excellent facilities in an idyllic setting – ideal for both learning and spiritual refreshment.

Unlock the secrets of abundant life

This eight-session resource will help you explore your deepest longings, motives and patterns of thinking and relating, and find deep security by drawing more thoroughly on the Father's love for you.
Suitable for group or individual use.

Designed for Living workbook

by Jeannette Barwick and Helena Wilkinson
96-page paperback, 148x210mm
ISBN: 978-1-85345-523-0

Find security in this insecure world

Examples of women in the Bible and women today plus some practical steps will lead to the lasting security found only in a relationship with God. Eight sessions for individual or group use.

How to be a Secure Woman workbook

by Jeannette Barwick and Catherine Butcher
96-page paperback, 148x210mm
ISBN: 978-1-85345-307-6

Live in harmony with the seasons of life

This six-session workbook for group or individual use looks at the way God leads us into times of activity and fulfilment as well as times of stillness and rest. Biblical studies, testimonies and questions will help you to live in harmony with the seasons of life.

Seasons – Embracing the rhythms of life

by Lynn Penson
96-page paperback, 148x210mm
ISBN: 978-1-85345-605-3

For current prices, more information or to order, visit **www.cwr.org.uk**
Also available in Christian bookshops